Kabīr and the Kabīr Panth

Kabir and the Kabir Panth

Kabir as represented in the picture hung in the Kabir Charan
Math, Benaras   *(Facing p. iii)*

Kabīr and the
Kabīr Panth

Rev. G.H. Westcott, M.A.

***Munshiram Manoharlal
Publishers Pvt. Ltd.***

ISBN 81-215-0000-1

Second revised edition 1986
Originally published in 1907
by Christ Church Mission Press, Cawnpore

Published and printed by Munshiram Manoharlal Publishers Pvt. Ltd.,
Post Box 5715, 54 Rani Jhansi Road, New Delhi-110055.

Contents

CHAPTER 7

The Teaching of the Panth 84

Glossary 103

Index 108

Illustrations

Preface

THE following pages represent the result of inquiries extending over the last ten years. The gradual way in which such information, as is given, has been acquired and the number of times that first impressions have had to give way to subsequent discoveries would be sufficient warning that this representation of the subject is little likely to be free from errors. My hope is that this study will do something to increase the interest already felt by many in the various religious sects that have been called into existence in India through the efforts of distinguished teachers.

I have tried to avoid dogmatising on questions that call for fuller investigation; but we have at any rate in the teaching of Kabīr an attempt to break down the barriers that separate Hindus from Muhammadans, and we have probably in the Kabīr Panth a religious system that owes something to Hindu, Muhammadan and Christian influences.

If Christ had been an Indian, would not his Gospel have been welcomed by many who now, refuse to listen?

For help in this undertaking I am principally indebted to my Mali, Badlu Dass, who is himself a member of the Panth. He has visited all places of interest in connexion with the Panth, has introduced me to many Mahants and conducted inquiries with great intelligence. The Rev. Ahmad Shah, who is now engaged in bringing out an edition of the *Bijak*, has made many valuable suggestions and has also superintended the copying of various Kabir Panthi manuscripts. Mr. U.R. Clement and the Rev. Prem Chand have also rendered valuable assistance, while the Rev. B.H.P. Fisher of this Mission has kindly seen these pages through the press.

S P.G. Mission House
Cawnpore

G.H. Westcott

Chronological Table

Century AD	Hindu	Christian
1100	Ramanuja 1090-1150 (?)	
1200		
1300	Ramanand 1300-1400 (?)	Wyckliffe 1324-84 Jordanus 1321
1400	Gorakh Nath 1420-85 (?)	Erasmus 1467-1536
	Kabir 1440-1518	Luther 1483-1546
	Nanak 1469-1538	Cranmer 1489-1555
	Chaitanya 1486-1527	
1500	Vallabha Swami 1520	Fr Xavier 1506-1552
	Dadu 1544-1603	J. Xavier goes to Lahore 1596
	Tulsi Dass 1544-1624	

Sankaracharya was born in AD 788 and died in AD 828.

CHAPTER 1

The Life of Kabīr

IT is generally allowed that of all the great Hindū Reformers Kabīr and Tulsī Dāss have had the greatest influence for good among the uneducated classes of Northern and Central India. Kabīr has been fittingly described by Sir W.W. Hunter as the Indian Luther of the 15th century.

Among those who acknowledge their indebtedness to Kabīr as a spiritual guide are Nānak Shāh of the Punjab, the founder of the Sikh community; Dādū of Ahmedabad (1544)[1] founder of the Panth that bears his name, and Jag Jīwan Dāss of Oudh (1760) the founder of the Sat Nāmī sect. Among religious teachers whose doctrine is said to be largely based upon the teaching of Kabīr are Bribhan, the founder of the Sādh community (1658), Bābā Lāl of Mālwā and Shivā Narāin of Ghazipur.

Of these Nānak Shāh is the teacher with whose name the English reader is most familiar and it is therefore well in his case to enlarge somewhat upon a bald assertion of indebtedness.

In the *Janam Sākhī*[2] Kabīr is mentioned as a Bhagat equal in merit to Nānak himself, and other Bhagats are exhorted to follow his example. On more than one occasion Nānak quotes with emphasised approval verses attributed to Kabīr.

The *Ādi Granth,*[3] the sacred book of the Sikhs, gives much information concerning the life of Kabīr and the character of his teaching. The interest which Nānak felt in Kabīr was probably

---

[1] All the dates given in the text refer to the year Anno Domini.

[2] *Jaman Sāktī* (Evidence or story of birth) is the name given to the accounts of Nānak, current among his followers. A translation of two such accounts will be found in Trumpp's edition of the *Ādi Granth.*

[3] *Ādi* first principal, *Granth* book. The term is used *Granth* by several sects to denote their authoritative writings.

The quotations from the *Ādi Granth* are taken from Trumpp's translation.

enhanced by the fact that he had enjoyed personal intercourse with the reformer.[1]

In modern days the number of those who have in one way or another come under the influence of Kabīr is very great. In the Census Report for 1901 the number of Kabīr Panthīs alone is returned as 843,171 and the actual number is probably considerably larger, as in the United Provinces, many Kabīr Panthīs seem to have been returned as Rāmānandīs and the figures for the Panjab are not included.[2]

There is no doubt as to the greatness of Kabīr's influence as a religious teacher; he has also been described as the founder of Hindī literature. The hymns of Kabīr are still sung by many a wandering minstrel, while his pithy sayings are frequently to win the attention of a dreamy audience or to clench a lengthy argument.

Unfortunately the material for a life of Kabīr is miserably scanty. If we confine our attention to traditions of historical value, we are left in uncertainty as to the place and date of his birth, his name, the religion to which he was attached by birth, the state of life in which he lived, married or single, and the number of years that he resided in any particular place. It is true that many legends have gathered round his name, but however interesting these may be from various points of view they can hardly be said to meet the needs of those who desire accurate information.[3]

It is admitted by all Kabīr Panthīs that Kabīr was brought up as a child in the house of Nīrū, a Muhammadan weaver. In the *Janam Sākhi* Nānak is reported to have told Bābar that Kabīr was a Muhammadan weaver. In the *Ādi Granth* occur these lines :

---

[1]Nānak is said to have been 27 years of age when he met Kabīr. As Nānak was born in 1469 the year of meeting will have been 1496, the very year in which Sikandar Lodi, the Emperor of Delhi, visited Jaunpur and other cities in that neighbourhood.

[2]This total is distributed as follows : Central Provinces, 493,393 : United Provinces, 15, 771; Central India 124,600; Bombay Presidency, 9,407.

[3]It is stated in the *Benares Gazetteer* that Kabīr was born at Belhara, a village in the district of Azamgarh. According to the belief of Kabīr Panthīs he was born in 1398 and died in 1518. The latter date is probably correct; the former is probably dictated by a desire to make him contemporaneous with Rāmānand who is supposed to have lived in the fourteenth century.

By caste a weaver and patient of mind: utters Kabīr with natural ease the excellencies of Rām.[1]

In one of his best known Hymns Kabīr says that he will shortly give up weaving and devote himself entirely to singing the praises of Hari.[2] In another hymn he says that he had in a previous birth been born as a Brahmin, but had been reincarnated as a *Julāhā* (Muhammadan weaver) because he had in that life neglected the worship of Rām (*Rām Bhajan*).

In none of the writings that can be traced directly to Kabīr is any account given as to the manner of his birth, but the following legends have long been current in this country:

The first legend relates that his mother was a Brahmin widow who went with her father on a pilgrimage to the shrine of a famous ascetic. To reward the devotion of the pilgrims the ascetie prayed that the woman might become the mother of a son. The prayer of so holy a man could not fail to find fulfilment and in due course the Brahman widow became the mother of Kabīr. The mother to escape dishonour exposed the infant, who was discovered and adopted as her own by the wife of a weaver.[3]

According to another version of this story Rāmānand, who was the ascetic referred to, said that he could not recall his blessing but would arrange that the birth should not be after the usual manner, but that the infant should issue from the palm of its mother's hand.[4] His promise was realised and the infant after birth was placed on a lotus flower in the midst of the Lahār Tank. It was there discovered by Nimā, the wife of Nīrū, and by her taken to her husband's house.

[1] In such passages Kabīr seems to apply the name Rām to the supreme God and not to the incarnation of Viṣṇu. He writes in the *Bijak* that the true Master did not take birth in the family of Dasrath.

[2] Kabīr likens the process of birth, death and re-birth to the movements of the shuttle. This passage may be interpreted as the expression of a hope that he will shortly obtain deliverance from the trials of transmigration.

[3] Most of the legends contained in this chapter are taken from a Hindi pamphlet entitled *Kabīr Kasauti*, published at Bombay in 1885. This pamphlet is the joint production of five members of the Kabīr Panth and is based upon information gleaned both from books and oral tradition.

[4] This legend enables the Hindu section of the Panth to explain the name Kabīr as a corruption of Kar-Bīr or the hero (born from) the hand (of a Brahmin woman).

The second account is more poetical in character and runs thus:

Kabīr descended from heaven to earth.[1] The lotus flower was blooming in the place where Kabīr was born. The bees were tired of humming. Peacocks, larks and other kinds of birds in their flight passed circling round the tank. Thunder and lightning were in the air when Kabīr became manifest in the heart of a lotus flower, in the midst of the Lahār tank. A feeling of thirst overcame Nimā, the newly wedded wife of Nīrū, the weaver as after the marriage ceremony she was making her way to her husband's house. She approached the tank but was much afraid when there she beheld the child. She thought in her heart 'this is probably the living evidence of the shame of some virgin widow.' Nīrū suggested that they might take the child to their house, but Nimā at first demurred, thinking that such action might give rise to scandal. Women would ask, "Who is the mother of a child so beautiful that its eyes are like the lotus" ? However laying aside all fears they took pity on the child. On approaching the house they were welcomed with the songs of women, but when the women saw the child dark thoughts arose in their hearts and they began to ask "How has she got this child"? Nimā replied that she had got the child without giving birth to it and the women then refrained from asking further questions.

The mystery surrounding the birth of the child was further deepened when Nīrū called in a Qāzī[2] and requested him to open a *Qorān*[3] and find for the child a name. He found the name Kabīr, and also from the same root, Akbar, Kubrā and Kibriyā. On finding these names the Qāzī was much perplexed and bit his nails, for was not the term Kabīr a title applied to God ? News of what had taken place soon spread, and after a short while five or six more Qāzīs arrived upon the scene. All opened the *Qorān*, but with the same result. They closed the book in silent astonishment. It was impossible, they all agreed, that a title of such dignity should be given as a name to a weaver's child. They opened the *Qorān* again and found the names, Zindā, Khinjar, Pīr and Haqqā. Thereupon they said to Nīrū, 'You must in some way destroy this child.'

---

[1] In the *Kabīr Kasauti* this phrase occurs—*Sewak hokar utre hai Pirthiwimanhi* "becoming a servant he descended upon this earth".

[2] Qāzi, a Muhammadan judge, whose services are requisitioned in connexion with births, marriages and other legal matters.

[3] In the *Qorān*, Sura Mariam, the infant Juses is represented as addressing those who were perplexed as to the nature of his birth, saying "Verily, I am the servant of God etc." See *Studies in Qorān* by Rev. Ahmad Shah, p. 106.

Nīrū in obedience to their order took the child within the house to put him to death, but before he had time to carry out his intention the child gave utterance to this *Shabda*:

"I have come from an unknown place. Māyā has deceived the world; no one knows me. I was not born of a woman, but manifested as a boy. My dwelling was in a lonely spot nigh to Kāsī,[1] and there the weaver found me. I contain neither heaven (air) nor earth, but wisdom only. I have come to this earth in spiritual form and of spiritual significance is my name. I have neither bones nor blood nor skin. I reveal to men the *shabda* (word). My body is eternal. I am the highest being. These are the words of Kabīr who is indestructible."

Thus were the Qāzīs defeated in their object and the name Kabīr was given to the child.[2]

As a boy Kabīr gave great offence to both Hindū and Muhammadan playmates. When in the course of play he cried out "Rām, Rām" and "Hari, Hari," the Muhammadans called him a *kāfir* (unbeliever). To this charge he retorted that he only was a *kāfir* who did evil. One day he put a *tilak* on his forehead and a *jāneo* round his neck and cried out "Nārain, Nārain." This action roused the ire of the Brahmins, since they regarded it as an infringement of their privileges. To their protest he objected:

"This is my faith, my tongue is Viṣṇu, my eyes are Nārain, and Gobind resides in my heart. What account will you give of your actions after death ? Being a weaver, I wear a thread. You wear the sacred thread, and repeat the *Gāyatrī* and *Gītā* daily, but Gobind dwells in my heart. I am a sheep, you are shepherds; it is your duty to save us from sin. You are Brahmins, I am a weaver of Benares. Hear my wisdom. You daily search after an earthly king, while I am contemplating Hari."[3]

He was further taunted with being a *nigura*, one without the benefit of a spiritual guide. He was determined to remove what he, as well as they, regarded as a reproach. He desired to become the *chelā* (disciple) of Rāmānand but felt that there were difficulties in the way which could only be overcome by means of some artifice.

[1]Kāsī, the Hindu name for Benares.
[2]For further comments on this legend see chapter 2.
[3]*Adi Granth*, Trumpp's translation, p. 661.

He knew that if only he could gain possession of the *mantra* peculiar to this sect, his initiation must necessarily follow. He learnt that Rāmānand regularly visited a certain bathing *ghāt* and determined to lie down upon the steps of that *ghāt* in the hope that Rāmānand might step on him by accident. His hope was realised and the holy man in his astonishment exclaimed "Rām, Rām." Kabīr knew that no words would rise so readily to the lips of this holy man as the *mantra* of his order and so claimed that as he was already in possession of the *mantra* he could no longer be refused admission to the order.[1]

When Kabīr announced that he had become the chelā of Rāmānand, both Hindus and Muhammadans were dismayed and a joint deputation went to inquire of Rāmānand whether it were true that he had received a Muhammadan boy as one of his disciples. Rāmānand asked them to produce the boy. The people took Kabīr to him. Rāmānand on his arrival raised the curtain which screened him from the public gaze and asked the boy when he had made him his disciple. Kabīr answered, "Various are the *mantras* that Gurūs whisper into the ears of their disciples, but you struck me on the head and communicated to me the name of Rām." The *Swāmi* recalled the circumstance, and drawing aside the curtain elasped him to his breast and said, "Beyond all questioning you became my disciple." The members of the deputation returned home disappointed. Kabīr returned to the weaver's house and set to work on the loom. When any Sādhu came to the house he used to have the ground prepared after the manner of Hindus and got food cooked for them in vessels not previously used. He himself would wait upon them while they took their food. His mother, Nimā, was annoyed at these proceedings which, she said, were not in accordance with the customs of the family.

From the time of his initiation Kabīr is said to have regularly visited his Gurū and, as years went on, to have taken part in religious disputations with distinguished Pandits who came to do battle with his master. According to tradition Kabīr was not possessed of any great amount of booklore, but in any case he must

---

[1]Kabīr Panthīs in conversation speak of their *mantra* as "Rām Rām," but it is a mistake to suppose that these words constitute the *mantra* either of their Panth or of the Rāmānandis. These *mantra* may not be disclosed to the uninitiated.

have gained through instruction, conversation and participation in religious disputations a considerable knowledge of Hindu philosophical thought and familiarity with such questions as arose out of the meeting of Hindu with Muhammadan beliefs.

It appears from legends of uncertain date that he continued to work as a weaver, giving part of his earnings to Nīrū and spending the rest in charity and more especially in giving food to Sādhus. Stories are told as to how on several occasions he mysteriously disappeared for a while from his father's house and in miraculous ways supplied the needs of others.

By some Kabīr is said to have been married to a woman, named Loī, and to have had by her two children, a son Kamāl and a daughter Kamāli. The circumstances which gave rise to this conjecture are thus related in *Kabīr Kasauṭī*.

One day Kabīr when he was some thirty years of age was walking along the bank of the Ganges when he came to a cottage belonging to a *Bankhandi Bairāgī*.[1] He went up to the cottage and there sat down. After some time a girl, about twenty years of age, also arrived. To her question as to who he was, Kabīr replied 'I am Kabīr.' She again inquired as to his caste and sect (*bhesh*). To both questions he returned the same answer, 'Kabīr'. The girl observed that though many Sants had come to that place none of them had ever given such a name for themselves, their caste or sect. Kabīr said that in saying this she had said what was perfectly true.[2] Meanwhile more Sants arrived. Presently the girl brought forth from the house a large supply of milk which she divided into seven shares. Five shares she gave to the Sants, one to Kabīr and the remaining share she kept for herself. Kabīr placed his share on the ground. The Sants drank theirs and asked Kabīr why he also did not drink his. Kabīr replied that he was keeping it for a Sādhu, now on his way, travelling from the other side of the Ganges. The girl said, "Sir, drink your share, I have plenty left for him." Kabīr

---

[1]*Bankhandi* is an epithet applied to Bairagis who live in the *jangal*.

[2]The meaning of this legend appears to be that there is only one God and that all men are his servants and will one day be brought into close union with Him. Religious distinctions are therefore out of place. The religious reformer may have hoped that Hindus and Muhammadans would lay aside all prejudice and accept as a title for the one true God the comparatively unknown term, Kabīr (The Great One).

made answer "My food is the Word of God." (*Ham Shabda āhāri hain*). Shortly afterwards the Sādhu arrived and the milk was given to him. The Sants asked the girl (Loī) of her parentage and how she came to be living in so lonely a spot. Loī replied that she had no parents living, that she had been brought up by a Sant, but that now he too was dead and she was living alone. They inquired the name of the Sant and the circumstances under which she had come to be living with him.

The girl, Loī, replied. "The Sant was a *Bankhandi Bairāgi* and he lived on milk alone. In reply to questions concerning me he used to say, 'I was bathing one day in the Ganges when a basket struck against me. I opened the basket and found in it a female infant. I took the infant to my home and reared it by means of a wick soaked in milk. Having found the infant wrapt in clothes I gave it the name of Loī (blanket). Such is the account that the Swāmī would give to the Sants."

Loī having observed the gravity of Kabīr said to him. "Swāmī, give me such teaching as will bring me peace of mind." Kabīr was pleased with the obvious sincerity of the girl and instructed her thus, "Always repeat *Satya Nām* (the true name) and spend your days in the service of the Sants." In obedience to this teaching she laid aside all worldly thoughts, went to Kāsī and passed her time in the service of the Sants. Nimā thought that Kabīr had brought home with him a wife and asked for what purpose he had married her as they did not live together as husband and wife.

On another occasion Kabīr was walking along the bank of the Ganges, accompanied by Shaikh Taqqī, when the latter suddenly caught sight of the dead body of a child floating down the stream. The Shaikh suggested that Kabīr should call the child. Kabīr whispered something into its ears, whereupon it at once began to weep. Shaikh Taqqī allowed that Kabīr had worked a miracle. On account of its beauty Kabīr named the child *Kamāl* (perfection) and made it over to Loī who reared it. The child regarded Loī as its mother and others seeing the child in Loī's lap regarded Kabīr as a married man.

Some time afterwards Kabīr happened to be in the house of a neighbour when his infant daughter died. Kabīr sought permission to remove the dead body to his house. The mother, who had heard how he had brought Kamāl back to life, after some persuasion induced the father to give his consent. Kabīr recalled the child

to life by means of *Shabda*, called her Kamāli and made her over
to Loī to be reared. Both children worked at the loom and addressed Kabīr as *Swāmījī*.

One day when Kamāli was now twenty years of age she happened to be drawing water at a well, when a Pandit came up and
asked for a drink. Having quenched his thirst he asked whose
daughter she was. He was greatly horrified when he learnt that she
was the daughter of a weaver and exclaimed 'You have broken my
caste.' Kamāli was at a loss to understand for what reason he had
become so angry, and persuaded him to come and discuss matters
with Kabīr. Before either had had time to explain matters, Kabīr
who could read the thoughts of men's hearts. exclaimed, "Before
drinking water think on these things. What is defilement ? Fishes,
tortoises. blood, salt, rotten leaves and the carcases of dead animals are all to be found in water. Crores of men have been slain
by Kāl; at every step you take, you tread upon the dead body of
some man and yet from such earth the vessels from which you
drink are made. At meal times you take off your clothes for fear of
defilement and wrap yourself in a *dhotī* that has been woven by a
weaver. The fly that visits the dunghill settles on your food. How
can you prevent this ? Dispel such illusions from the mind, study
the Vedas and take refuge in Rām."

At the Pandit's request Kabīr gave him further instruction in the
doctrine of *Satya Nām* and gave him Kamāli in marriage.

The plain speaking of Kabīr and his general disregard for the
conventions of society raised him up enemies on every side. According to Kabīr Panthi traditions it was Shaikh Taqqi who voiced the
feelings of Muhammadans,[1] This famous Pīr came before the
Emperor, Sikandar Lodi and accused Kabīr of laying claim to
Divine attributes. He urged that such conduct merited the penalty
of death. The Emperor issued a warrant for his arrest and sent
men to bring him to the court. Not till evening could the men who
were sent persuade Kabīr to accompany them. Kabīr stood before
the Emperor in silence. The Qāzi exclaimed, "Why do you not
salute the Emperor, you *kāfir* ?" Kabīr replied, "Those only are
Pirs who realise the pains of others, those who cannot are *kāfirs*."
The Emperor asked him why, when ordered to appear in the morn-

---

[1]On chronological and other grounds it seems highly improbable that Shaikh
Taqqi played the part assigned to him in this legend. See chapter 2.

ing, he had not come till evening. Kabīr replied that he had seen a
sight which arrested his attention. The Emperor asked what kind
of a sight could justify him in disregarding his commands. Kabīr
rejoined that he had been watching a string of camels passing
through a street narrower than the eye of a needle. The Emperor
said that he was a liar. Kabīr replied, "O Emperor, realise how
great is the distance between heaven and earth. Innumerable
elephants and camels may be contained in the space between the
sun and the moon, and all can be seen through the pupil of the
eye which is smaller than the eye of a needle." The Emperor was
satisfied and let him go, but the people murmured and complained
that the Emperor had disregarded their complaints. Shaikh Taqqi
said that it was contrary to the teaching of the Prophet that a
man who claimed Divine powers should be allowed to live and
that Kabīr should suffer as Mansūr and Shams Tahrezi had suffered of old.[1]

The Brahmins added that he was *be-dharmi* because he had associated with a woman of ill fame and Rāe Dass, the *chamār*.[2] Kabīr
told the Emperor of his doctrine, but to no effect for he sided
with the people and gave orders that Kabīr should be put to death.
Kabīr was removed and made fast in chains. He was then placed
on board a boat which was filled with stones. The boat sank, but
Kabīr re-appeared as a boy, floating down the stream on a leo-
pard's skin.[3] He was again captured and now an attempt was
made to burn him alive. He was locked up in a hut which was
afterwards set on fire. When the flames were extinguished Kabīr
re-appeared in a form of great beauty. He was now accused of
witchcraft and the people demanded that he should be trampled

[1]Both these men were Sūfī saints. Mansūr was cruelly tortured and afterwards
hung for saying of himself "I am the Truth". Shams-ud-din Tabrezi was the
Murshid (spiritual director) of Jalāl-ud-din, famous as the author of the Masnavi.
He flourished about 1244. A short account of Mansur Al Halrāz (the cotton
carder) and Shāms Tabrezi, together with extracts from the latter's writings,
will be found in *The Persian Mystics*, Wisdom the East Series.

[2]The *Chamārs* are workers in leather and accounted of very low caste as
being associated in their work with the skins of dead animals. Several religious
reformers were men of low caste; Rae Dāss was a *chamār*; Senā a barber;
Dādū a cotton cleaner; Nābhāji, the author of the *Bhakt Māla*, a *dom* (sweeper).

[3]Bairagis often carry about the skin of a deer or other animal upon which
they take their seat upon the ground. It is symbolic of a life spent in places
apart from the haunts of men.

to death by an infuriated elephant. Between the elephant and Kabīr there appeared a lion, at the sight of which the elephant took fright.[1] Finally the Emperor asked forgiveness of Kabīr and expressed his willingness to undergo any punishment that he might name. To this Kabīr replied that a man should sow flowers for those who had sown him thorns.

The stories so far related speak of Kabīr as a resident of Kāsi (Benares). It is natural that his Hindu followers should wish to associate him as closely as possible with their sacred city, but there is evidence both from the *Bījak* and the *Ādi Granth* to show that he did not at any rate spend the whole of his life in Benares.

In the *Bījak* is found a *Ramaini* which may be interpreted thus :

"Kabīr settled for a while in Manikpur having heard of the praises of Shaikh Taqqi. He heard also about Uji in the district of Jaunpur. At Jhusi he heard the names of his Pīrs,[2] He heard of twenty-one Pīrs in all. They preach in the name of the Prophet. On hearing this I could not refrain from speaking. The people have looked on the shrines and gone astray. The works of Habibi (beloved) and Nabi (prophet) are all contrary to law (*harām*). O Shaikh Aqardi and Shaikh Saqardi, listen to my words. See the beginning as well as the end with open eyes, consider every period of the world's history."

In the opening lines of this Ramaini Kabīr seems to be enumerating the places which he had visited in his search for religious guidance : in the closing lines to be grieving over the thought that more honour is paid to the tombs of the dead than to the God in whose service their lives were spent.[3]

In the *Ādi Granth* these lines are put into the mouth of Kabīr.

My Hajj is on the banks of the Gomti : where dwells my Pīr, wearing a yellow robe.[4]

Reference is here apparently made to Jaunpur which is situated on the left or northern bank of the Gomti. Jaunpur was the capital of a famous Muhammadan (Sharqi) dynasty. Ibrahim, one of the kings of this dynasty (1412), was a great patron of Muhammadan

---

[1] See, Kabīr in History, under Shaikh Abdul Kabīr, p. 15.

[2] His Pīrs, *i.e.* Shaikh Taqqi and his father Shabān-ul-millat, who were always closely associated together.

[3] For further comments upon this *Ramaini* see chapter 2.

[4] Muhammadan Pīrs wear yellow garments.

learning, but was in this respect surpassed by Bībī Rājah, who built a magnificent Jami Mosque, a College and a Monastery. She also appropriated large sums of money for the maintenance of those learned in Theology and the Sciences. With the exception of the Mosque all these buildings were subsequently destroyed by Sikandar Lodi either on religious or political grounds.[1]

We gather from this quotation that Kabīr was born elsewhere than in Jaunpur, but that he received religious instruction in that city.

There are many other stories connected with the life of Kabīr, but we will only reproduce one more before passing on to consider the manner of his death. This story is of interest as it associates Kabīr with Central India where at the present time his influence is most strongly left.

There lived in the Deccan two brothers, Tatvā and Jivā, who were anxious to find for themselves a spiritual guide. They used religiously to wash the feet of the many Sādhus who visited their house and listened attentively to their teaching. At a loss to discover which of these Sādhus were possessed of real spiritual power they devised the following test. They planted in the courtyard of their house a withered branch of a banyān tree and agreed to accept as their Guru that Sādhu whose power was such, that the washings of his feet would avail to restore the branch to life. For forty years they waited in vain for one who could satisfy the test and were almost in despair of ever finding the desired Guru, when Kabīr arrived upon the scene. The branch when sprinkled with the water in which his feet had been washed immediately returned to life. Kabīr was accepted as their Guru and gave utterance to these lines : The Sādhus are my soul and I am the body of the Sādhus : I live in the Sādhus, as rain lives in the clouds.

The Sādhus are my Ātmā, and I am the life of the Sādhus : I live in the Sādhus, as *ghi* lives in the milk. The Sādhus are my Ātmā and I am the bread of the Sādhus : I live in the Sādhus as fragrance lives in the flowers.

All accounts agree that the earthly life of Kabīr came to a close at Maghar in the district of Gorakhpur. We are not told whether

---

[1]Jaunpur is said to be a corruption of Javanpur. *Javan* a term applied originally to the Greeks, was subsequently applied to the Muhammadans. The meaning of Jaunpur would therefore be the city of Muhammadans.

he had ever previously visited this place, but he may possibly have done so when on a visit to Gorakh Nāth, the famous Yogi and founder of the Shivite sect that bears his name.

There are lines in the *Ādi Granth* in which Kabīr refers to the austerities practised by Gorakh Nāth and speaks of him as having died in spite of all.[1]

Tradition relates that Kabīr died in extreme old age. when his body had become infirm and his hands were no longer able to produce the music with which he had in younger days celebrated the praises of Rām. If he had lost the company of earthly friends he felt more closely united, than ever before, to one from whom he would never more be parted. Such appear to be the thoughts which find expression in the following lines, quoted from the *Ādi Granth*:

> Benares has been left by me and my intellect has become little, my whole life is lost in Shivpuri, at the time of death I have arisen and come to Maghar.
>
> O my king, I am a Bairāgi and Yogi : when dying, I am not grieved, nor separated from Thee.
>
> The mind and breath are made the drinking gourd, the fiddle is constantly prepared : the string has become firm, it does not break, unbeaten the fiddle sounds.[2]
>
> Sing, sing, O bride, a beautiful song of blessing: King Rām, my husband, has come to my house.

It was the wish of his disciples 'that Kabīr should end his days at Kāsi where so much of his religious work had been accomplished. All who died in Kāsi, they urged, would pass immediately into the presence of Rām, while those who died at Maghar would return to this world and assume the form of an ass. Kabīr rebuked them for their want of faith. Is the power of Rām so limited that he cannot save his servant because he prefers to die outside Kāsi, the city of Shivā ?

---

[1] Gorakh Nāth and another Hindu ascetic, Machhendar, who is more than once referred to in the *Bijak*, are also by tradition associated with Jhusi. See *Allahabad Gazetteer*, p. 190.

[2] In Kabīr literature the soul of man is often compared to a string. His soul is now attuned to sing the praises of God.

What Kāsi ? What Maghar ? He who dies at Maghar is not dead, when Rām has taken up his abode in my heart: he who dies elsewhere puts Rām to shame.

A difficulty arose with regard to the disposal of his body after death. The Muhammadans desired to bury it and the Hindus to cremate it. As the rival parties discussed the question with growing warmth Kabīr himself appeared and bade them raise the cloth in which the body lay enshrouded. They did as he commanded and lo ! beneath the cloth there lay but a heap of flowers ! Of these flowers the Hindus removed half and burnt them at Benares, while what remained were buried at Maghar by Muhammadans.[1]

Kabīr in History

The following abstracts from standard books of reference will suffice to show that the name "Kabīr" is not so rare as has sometimes been supposed. There is reason to question the accuracy of some of the dates[2] and reason to believe that some of Kabīr's biographers, working upon the assumption that there was only one Kabīr, have unhesitatingly appropriated details from the lives of several.

In *Khanzinat-ul-Asfiā* (Treasury of Saints)[3] written by Maulvi Gulam Sarwar and published at Lahore about 1868, mentioned is made of :

1. *Kabīr Chishiti*, Sufi and inhabitant of Nāgore who on account of ill-treatment at the hands of Muhammadans journeyed in the direction of Gujarat and died there in 1854.

[1] A very similar story is told in connexion with the death of Nānak. See Hughes, *Dictionary of Islam*, p. 588.

[2] Dates may have been transferred from the History of one man to that of another bearing the same name, or difficulty may have been experienced in deciphering dates written in Persian figures, without an accompanying verbal explanation.

[3] In this book Shaikh Taqqi is described as *Hayāk*, the Arabic equivalent of the Persian *Jullāhā*. He is said to have lived at Maṇikpur and to have died in 1574.

2. *Shaikh Kabīr Julāha*, the disciple and successor of Shaikh Taqqi, who is described as being one of the great men of his time and a leader among Theists. He is described as the author of many Hindi writings which prove him to have been a man of great ability. He taught the Sūfī doctrine of *Wisāl* (Union with God) and preserved silence with regard to the contrary doctrine of *Firāq* (separation). He is said to have been the first to write anything about God and his attributes in the Hindi language, and to have been the author of various Hindi poems. On account of his religious toleration he was accepted as a leader by Hindus as well as by Muhammadans and styled by the former *Pīr Kabīr* and by the latter *Bhagat Kabīr*. The date of his death is given as 1594.

3. *Khwājāh Auliā Kabīr* who visited Bokhārā and died in 1229.

4. *Syed Kabīr-ud-din Hassan* of the same family as Kabīr-ud-din Ismail, who is said to have travelled three times round the world and to have lived to the age of 180. He resided at Uch in Balakh near the birth place of Jalal-ud-din, where he died in 1490.

5. *Shaikh Kabīr*, the son of Shaikh Munawar and resident of Bajaora, who is simply described as a conceited man and a victim of the opium habit.

In *Sair-ul-Aqtab* (History of Pillar Saints), written by Shaikh Allah Diya; mention is made of?

6. *Shaikh Abdul Kabīr* who is said to have been a saint from his mother's womb and to have possessed a great power of foretelling events. He was known as *Shaikh Kabīr* or *Bālā Pir* and inherited the priestly robe of the Sūfīs from his father, Abdul Quddus. He performed many miracles and by merely shaking the sleeve of his robe was able to cause a lion to appear. He had a taste for singing and was lavish in his hospitality. He had four sons and many disciples. The king of Jaunpur, Sultan Sikandar Lodi, together with his Vizier, Bhudhā, and Malik Mahmūd determined to test his powers as a saint. It was arranged that they should visit him one evening, each having previously in his own mind thought of some particular dish. If the Pīr supplied the want of each he was to be regarded as a man of God. As soon as they entered his house Kabīr brought a dish of venison sandwiches and placed it before the king; to the Vizier he offered a bowl of soup and some bread and to Malik Mahmūd a dish of sweetmeats. The result was that his guests begged forgiveness for having ever called his powers in question. This Kabīr died in 1539. He is said

to have been succeeded by his son Shaikh Usmān, who was generally known as Zindā Pir.[1]

In *Muntākhab-ut-Tawārīkh* by Mullah Abdul Qādir of Budaon
mentioned is made of:

7. *Shaikh Kabīr*, a resident of Multān, who journeyed north-
wards to Balakh and returned from thence to India and travelled
in the company of Akbar, Owing to exhaustion brought on by the
severity of his devotions and night watches he is said to have
presented the appearance of a drunkard.

Mullāh Abdul Qadir himself met this saint at Fatehpur in 1585 AD.

In *Akhbār-ul-Akhyār* mention is made of :

8. *Amīr Kabīr Mīr Syed Ali Hāmdāni* who visited Kāshmīr in
1379 and died there five years later. After his death a dispute arose
concerning the disposal of his body between the people of Kāshmīr
Sultan Muhammad and Shaikh Aqwām-ud-din of Badakhshan.
The last named finally secured the body, but the people of Kāshmīr
erected a cenotaph at the place where he died.

In the Ferishtā mention is also made of :

9. Syed Ahmad Kabīr, the Fathea of Syed Jalāl-ud-din, and

10. *Kabīr-ud-din Ismail*, grandson, disciple and successor of
Syed Jalāl-ud-din, otherwise known as *Makhdum Jahanian* or *Jahān
Gusht Shūh* from the fact that he travelled extensively to Mecca,
Balakh etc. Kabīr-ud-din Ismail also travelled extensively and died
in 1421.

11. At Jaunpur there is a small Masjid, built in memory of Divān
Shāh Kabīr who was one of four brothers, all of whom lie buried
in the same plot of ground. This Masjid, which was built during
the reign of the Emperor Humayun, is situated in the Muhalla
Tār Talā.

---

[1]The name *Bālā Pīr* occurs in the list of the Mahants of the Dharam Dāss
section of the Kabīr Panth and the words *Zindā Pīr* in the legend of the naming
of Kabīr .

CHAPTER 2

The Life of Kabīr (*Contd.*)

THE traditional life of Kabīr has a poetical beauty which in its power to commend a Muhammadan Saint to Hindū followers may be thankfully regarded as a prophecy of the greater reconciliation of conflicting faiths to which so many of us look forward. The veil that has been drawn over the first beginnings of an important religious movement we would reverently raise, trusting thereby to add additional lustre to the brave efforts of a distinguished champion of religious truth.

H.H. Wilson, the distinguished Sanskrit scholar, to whose investigations every English student of Indian religious thought was so deep a debt of gratitude, writes of the improbability, not to say impossibility, of Kabīr's having been a Muhammadan, and with no more respect does he treat Col. Malcolm's suggestion that he belonged to the Sufi sect. Later writers have been content to yield to authority and to accept as established truth the judgement of a great scholar.

Did we believe that Wilson had carefully investigated all the documents that are now available to students, we should hardly presume to question the accuracy of his judgement, but we cannot help feeling that in the immensity of the tasks which he imposed upon himself he has overlooked some part of the evidence, or possibly too readily accepted the statements of fellow workers in the same field.

Any one who has read Wilson's account of Kabīr's life would carry away the impression that Nābhāji, the author of the *Bhakta Māla,* had recorded some at least of the legends which have found a place in the previous chapter. Nābhāji himself, to judge from the carefully printed edition of the *Bhakta Māla* now current in India, is only responsible for the following statement :

"Kabīr refused to acknowledge caste distinctions or to recognise the authority of the six schools of Hindu philosophy, nor did he set any store by the four divisions of life (*ashrām*) prescribed for Brahmins. He held that religion without Bhakti was no religion at all and that asceticism, fasting and almsgiving had no value if unaccompanied by worship (*bhajan*, hymn singing). By means of *Ramainīs, Shabdas* and *Sākhīs* he imparted religious instruction to Hindus and Muhammadans alike. He had no preference for either religion, but gave teaching that was appreciated by the followers of both. He spoke out his mind fearlessly and never made it his object merely to please his hearers."

This short account describes a man who had no great sympathy with Brahminical teaching, who believed in a personal God and in salvation by faith rather than by good works, and who delivered a message, regarded as God's message, to Hindūs and Muhammadans alike.

This is all that is stated in the text, but to the text is appended a commentary written by a later hand.[1] In this commentary it is stated that Kabīr in his desire to wear a *kanthi* round his neck and a *tilak* on his forehead (to attract a Hindu audience) made up his mind to become a disciple of Rāmānand and achieved his purpose as described in the chapter one[2]; that Muhammadans objected to the repetition 'Rām, Rām,' by a co-religionist and asked Rāmānand whether it were true that he had received a *julāhā* as his disciple; that Rāmānand at first denied that he had done so but when confronted with Kabīr acknowledged his mistake. Mention is also made of the fact that Kabīr was charged before the Emperor, Sikandar Lodi, and refused on that occasion to salute the Emperor, that he was sentenced to death and was in succession thrown into the Ganges, committed to the flames and exposed to the fury of an elephant, but all to no purpose. It is added that the emperor, thwarted in his desire to destroy Kabir recognised that he had acted wrongly, asked Kabir's forgiveness and offered to compensate him for the injuries inflicted.

[1]According to one account Nābhāji wrote his account of the *Bhagats* in Sanskrit and asked his disciple Priya Dāss to provide it with a commentary. Priyā made a beginning and then handed over the MS to Govardhan Nāth. Finally the commentary was completed by Narain Dāss, a disciple of Govardhan Nāth and published in 1769.

[2]We gather from the legend that Kabīr was received into the Rāmānandi Sect as a Hindū and that trouble arose subsequently when it was discovered that he was really a Muhammadan.

Nābhāji may have been acquainted with the legends now append- ed to his statement and his editor may have known of othe legends not recorded, but we have no right to assume such knowledge, nor are we yet in a position to say at what time other legends gradually became current. All that we know is that such are now to be found in various writings of unknown date, but accepted as authoritative by members of the Kabīr Panth.

We are inclined to accept both of the theories advanced by Col. Malcolm and to believe not only that Kabīr was a Muhammadan by birth but also that he was associated with the Sufi order; and that the great object of his life was to break down the barriers that separated Hindūs from Muhammadans. We believe that in his desire to achieve this object he actually took up his residence in Benares and associated there with the followers of Rāmānand. We can well imagine that his teaching gave offence both to orthodox Muhammadans and to orthodox Hindūs, and it is probable that both parties welcomed the opportunity afforded by Sikandar Lodi's visit to Jaunpur in 1495 to wait upon him with a request that he would rid them of one who despised tradition when in conflict with the truth.

Sikandar Lodi is represented by, Muhammadan historians as one who was zealous for the faith and had on one occasion put to death a distinguished Pandit, Jodhan by name, because he refused to allow that Islam had a monopoly of spiritual truth. Fortunately for Kabīr Muhammadan rulers were wont to allow Sūfis considera- ble license in their criticism of the faith, especially when such Sūfis combined personal piety with poetical talent. When we read how the enemies of Kabīr reminded the Emperor of the fate that had befallen Mansūr and Shāms Tabrezi who were both distinguished Sufi saints, we feel that they had some knowledge of this weakness and feared lest Kabīr might on such grounds escape the death penalty which alone would satisfy their embittered feelings. Their fears were realised, for we gather from the legend that the Emperor compromised the case; he spared the life of Kabīr, but banished him from the city where his teaching had given so great offence.

That Kabīr had been brought up in a Muhammadan family was probably a fact too well known to allow of contradiction. All that his Hindu followers could do was to suggest that he was not of Muhammadan origin, but only a Muhammadan by adoption. The name Kabīr was also too well established to allow of any alteration,

It only remained to explain its origin in a way that would commend itself to those who accepted the story of the virgin birth. Such an explanation was to be found in the fact that Al Kabīr is one of the 99 names of God in use among Muhammadans. The name Kabīr occurs in the Qorān six times as a title of Allah and once as a title of Al-Rabb.

The legend that calls attention to this fact presents a curious blend of Hindu and Muhammadan procedure. It is customary for Muhammadans to open a Qorān and give to the child the name on which the eye of the reader may first chance to fall; it is customary for Hindus to bestow upon a child a name containing three words usually beginning with the same letter and so similar in sound. This name is suggested by the position of the stars at the time of birth and is known as the *Rāsi* or astronomical name. The three names, Akbar, Kubrā and Kibriyā[1] said to have been found by the Qāzi in the Qorān are all derived from the same root KBR 'great'. Of these three names however only one, Kibriyā, is to be found in modern Qorāns. Of the three names Zinda, Khinjar and Pīr, the first and third are Persian words and as such not found in the Qorān. Khinjar is probably a corruption of Khizar the name of the saint who is in the Qorān associated with Moses.

A legend containing impossible details can hardly be regarded as a literal representation of historical fact.

Muhammadan tradition asserts that Kabīr had a son, Kamāl by name. This name also is of Arabic origin and so a source of difficulty to those who regard Kabīr as a Hindu *sādhu*. There is a word *kammal*, a corruption of *kambal* (blanket) and in one version of the Kamāl legend it is stated that Kabīr caught sight of the child floating down the stream, wrapt up in a blanket and cried out, not "Kamāl, Kamāl" but "Kammal, Kammal".

Muhammadan tradition implies that Kabīr like other Sūfi leaders was a married man, but as, in accordance with Muhammadan custom, no mention is made of his wife's name, Hindus were free to supply her with a Hindi name and chose Loi which also means a blanket.

There is a possible reference to his wife in the following lines contained in the *Ādi Granth*.

[1] The statement that of the names Akbar, Kubra, and Kibriya, Kibriya alone is to be found in modern Qorāns, is inaccurate. All three names are to be found. Akbar occurs 22 times, Kubra 6 times and Kibriya twice.

> The first wife was ugly, of low caste, of ill-boding feature :
> wicked in the house of her father-in-law and in her father's
> house;
> The present wife is beautiful, intelligent, of auspicious
> features, easily child-bearing.

These lines may be interpreted to mean that Kabīr has lost his
wife, but found comfort in closer union with God; or they may
mean that the soul at first united with a material body rejoiced in
the thought of becoming spiritually one with God.

In certain respects the legendary life of Kabīr presents remark-
able parallels to incidents in the life of Christ. After an account
of the virgin birth we read that Kabīr, as a boy, meets and worsts
in argument a learned Pandit; he is criticised for associating with
the outcasts of society; he miraculously supplies the poor with
bread; he incurs the hostility of the religious leaders of his time;
he raises from the dead a boy and a girl and is ministered to by
women. The full account of his appearance before Sikandar Lodi
presents in many details a striking resemblance to Christ's trial
before Pilate.

The books containing these legends are of comparatively late
date and the writers may have been influenced by a desire to
assimilate the life of Kabīr to that of Christ.

Many of the legends, especially some which have not been mentioned in this chapter seem to have originated in a desire to explain
the circumstances under which some of Kabīr's best known sayings
were first spoken, or to associate the memory of Kabīr with
persons and institutions held in special reverence by Hindus.
Several appear in different forms and nearly all contain details
which must raise difficulties in the minds of all who are not
overcredulous.

In the Dabistān, a Persian history, said to have been written by
Mohsin Fani of Kashmir in the reign of Akbar, it is stated that
Kabīr was a weaver and a Muwāhid i.e. a believer in one God. It
is further stated that in his desire to find spiritual guidance he
visited Muslim as well as Hindu sages, and finally became a disciple of Rāmānand under the circumstances already recorded in
this legend. Mention is also made of the following story :

One day when certain Brahmans were expatiating on the purify-
ing qualities of the Ganges water, Kabīr filled his wooden cup with

water from the river and offered it to them to drink. They were
horrified at the thought of drinking out of the cup belonging to a
low caste man; upon which Kabīr remarked, "If the Ganges water
cannot purify my cup, how can I believe that it can wash away my
sins ?"

The statement that Kabīr was a Julāhā and Muwāhid is confirmed by Abdul Fazl and has never been contradicted. What we
have to determine is the exact meaning of the statement. Hindus
have assumed that Kabīr in early life actually followed the frofes-
sion of a weaver and have quoted his use of weaving metaphors by
way of illustration. This he may have done, but we must also bear
in mind that it was customary for Muhammadans of that age to
attach to their personal names the name of the profession with
which their family had originally been associated. The term Muwāhid was not, so far as I can learn, ever applied by Muhammadans
those whom they regarded as idolater. It implies that he was a
to theist and not a pantheist. The prevailing impression that Kabīr
was a Pantheist appears, to be based upon two false assumptions,
(1) that he is responsible for all the teaching given by his Hindu
followers at a later age and (2) that all the statements contained
in the *Bijak* represent his personal views. There is reason to believe
that insufficient care has been taken in studying the context in
which certain sayings occur; reason to fear that Kabīr has been
credited with the argument of Māyā whom he at all times ruthlessly
condemns.

Great interest attaches to the mention of Shaikh Taqqi. According to the Hindu legends Shaikh Taqqi was the rival and opponent
of Kabīr while Muhammadans regard him as his Pīr. In the
Ramaini quoted in the chapter. One there is probably a reference
to two Shaikh Taqqis whom later writers have not been always
careful to distinguish.

Shaikh Taqqi of Mānikpur Karā was a *najāf* (cotton cleaner)
by profession and belonged to the Chistia order of Sūfis He is said
to have died at Bhandārpur in 1545 but there is probably some
mistake about the date. In the *Aina Oudh* it is stated that this
Shaikh Taqqi was the disciple and successor of Shaikh Nathan
Dānā who himself succeeded Shaikh Khwājah Kargh and that the
last named died in 1305. Shaikh Taqqi was succeeded by his son
Makān who founded a village in the Fatehpur district which is
called after him Mākanpur. His descendants are still to be found in

that and the neighbouring villages. From the statement contained in the *Ramaini* it appears that Kabīr visited Mānikpur and remained there for some time in attendance upon the Shaikh or his successors.

The Mānikpur referred to is situated on the Northern bank of the Ganges, between Fatehpur and Allahabad. It was for a short time the Military headquarters of the Emperor Sikandar Lodi. Near Mānikpur, but on the Southern bank of the river is Karā generally known as Karā Mānikpur, at that time a city of considerable importance, the Muhammadan capital of the surrounding country Karā.

Karā Mānikpur is the headquarters of a sect, called Malūk Dāssis. Members of this sect when on pilgrimage to Jagannath are required to visit the Math of the Kabīr Panthis and to receive there *Kabīr ka Tarāni* which consists of a piece of bread and a spoonful of sour rice water.[1]

At the same time it would seem that Kabīr was more closely associated with Shaikh Taqqi of Jhūsī[2] or his successors in office. This Shaikh was the son of Shaban-ul-Millat and belonged to the Soharwardiā order of Sūfis. He died in 1429 (AH 785) and his tomb at Jhūsī is still a place of pilgrimage.[3] Kabīr is said to have been a young man of about 30 years of age when he first made the acquaintance of the Shaikh. At the time he desired to have as his Pir one whose hand would ever remain over him to protect him from all evil. Shaikh Taqqi promised to help him in this way and proved true to his word, for even in the remote regions of Balkh[4] and Bokhārā Kabīr saw the protecting hand of his Pīr stretched over him as that of a guardian angel.[5] When Kabīr returned from

---

[1]Malūk Dāss is said to have been born in 1574. The *Granth* of this sect includes *Gyān Dīpak. Sukh Nidhān* and *Malūk Dāss ki Bhakti.* The two first are Kabīr Panth writings. See Wilson, *Religious Sects of the Hindus,* p. 102.

[2]Jhūsi stands near the confluence of the Ganges and the Jumna, in the immediate neighbourhood of Allahabad.

[3]In the *Aina Oudh* the father of Shaikh Taqqi is said to have been born in 1261.

[4]Balakh in north Afghanistān was the birth-place of Jalāl-ud-din Rumi, the author of the *Masnawi.* It is for Sūfis a place of pilgrimage. Kabīr is said to have visited Balakh. The name also occurs in the title of two Kabīr writings, *Balakh* and *Balakh kī Ramaini.*

[5]The people of Jhūsi were not sure that Kabīr actually visited those distant lands. They thought it possible that he merely closed his eyes and visited them in imagination.

his wanderings and repaired to Jhūsi to pay his respects to his Master he felt the pangs of hunger and asked that he might have some food. The Shaikh provided him with some vegetables, cooked rice and some skimmed milk spiced with caraway seeds. Kabīr regarded these supplies as inadequate to the occasion and exclaimed :

> Sāg, bhāt, jirwāni māthā
> Hamre Pīr ke yehi hātā.

Vegetable, rice, skimmed milk spiced with caraway :
These things only can be had in the market of my Pīr.
The Shaikh was vexed with his ingratitude and replied :

> Yih chhor aur kyā khāh hai māti,
> Toh upar pare che mās ki tāti.

Beside this what would you eat, earth ?
May six months motion disease come over you.

As the result of this curse Kabīr for six months suffered severely from attacks of diarrhoea. He rolled on the ground in agony and the two empty water courses in which he was then compelled to pass his time are still to be seen, the one bearing the name of Kabīr Nālā and the other that of Lotan Nālā. At the end of six months he was once more permitted to approach his Pīr. He apologized for his past ingratitude and received a blessing from his Master. Kabīr besought the Shaikh to bestow upon him such a blessing that he might be enabled to remove those differences of belief which separated Hindus from Muhammadans. Shaikh Taqqi regretted that this lay beyond his power, but said that he would bring it about that both Hindus and Muhammadans should regard Kabīr himself with reverence. Kamāl, the son of Kabīr when he heard of his father's request went to Shaikh Taqqi and requested him as his Pīr to release him from all further obligations to his father for he could never bring himself to look with favour upon Hindus. The Shaikh gave Kamāl permission to go and settle at Jalālpur, some ten miles distant from Jhusi.

Kabīr was sorrowful when he learnt of his son's determination and exclaimed:

Dubba bans Kabīr kā upjā pūt Kamāl

The family of Kabīr became extinct when his son Kamāl was born.[1]

Previous to the mutiny there was at Jhusi a large Mosque, associated with the memory of Shaikh Taqqi and endowed with landed property, bringing in an annual income of Rs. 100,000. After the mutiny the mosque was destroyed and the lands confiscated.[2]

The various allusions to persons and places contained in the *Ramaini* quoted in the previous chapter have been a great cause of perplexity to Hindu readers of the *Bijak*. Manikpur they explained as being the city of the *man* (mind). Of Uji, a village near Kharaunā in the district of Jaunpur, famous of old as the residence of some distinguished Muhammadan saint, they had never heard. When the people of Jhusi were asked about the 'Ikkis Pīr, (twenty one Pīr) they at once made mention of the Akelā Peṛ (solitary tree), a large tree that stands alone and under which a Muhammadan saint used to take up his abode. The promptness of their reply suggested that the original text might have been emended by some Hindu who had never heard of the Akelā Peṛ. Shaikh Aqardi and Shaikh Saqardi who became a still greater cause of perplexity were according to local tradition the Mujāwar or caretakers of Shaikh Taqqi's shrine, who were regarded by the people with so great respect that they were popularly known as Shaikhs.

We have probably written enough to show that it is not impossible that Kabīr should have been both a Muhammadan and a Sūfi. The picture of Kabīr which forms the frontispiece of this volume and which is more likely to have been painted by a Hindu than by a Muhammadan represents him as having Muhammadan features, and his grave at Maghar has always been in the keeping of Muhammadans. That a Muhammadan should have been the Father of Hindi literature may indeed be a cause of surprise, but it must not be forgotten that Hindus also have gained distinction of writers of Persian poetry. Kabīr, moreover, was a man of no ordinary ability and determination, and the purpose of his life was to get his message accepted by those who were best reached through the Hindi language.

[1] A similar saying occurs in the *Ādi Granth*: The progeny of Kabīr dead; there was born a son Kamāl. Having given up the remembrance of Hari, he has brought wealth to the house.

[2] Most of the information concerning Jhūsi traditions was supplied by Shah Fida Hussain, Government pensioner, resident in Jhusi.

CHAPTER 3

The Teaching of Kabīr

IN the days of Kabīr the power of the Brahmins was very great. As some would express it, the whole land was overcast by the dark clouds of priestcraft and sacerdotalism. Brahmanism, invigorated by its triumph over Buddhism, asserted its authority over all, until the Muhammadans invaded the country and gradually extended their influence throughout Northern India. Then people saw that there were men whose views about religion were radically different from those of their own Pandits; they became acquainted with men who were only with difficulty restrained on political grounds from exterminating all who refused to acquiesce in their own religious beliefs.

We are not in a position to say how far religious thinkers were encouraged by the presence of Muhammadans to give expression to the thoughts of their hearts, but there is no doubt that the presence of the followers of Islam stimulated thought on such subjects as caste, spiritual birth and the personality of God. Among the Muhammadans none were more ready than the Sūfis to recognise the good in every form of belief and to dwell upon the love of God towards all his creatures.

Before considering the character of Kabir's teaching we have first to determine what his teaching was. It seems probable that the teaching of Kabir was delivered orally and not reduced to writing till a later age. The earliest writings in which his teaching is recorded are the *Bijak* and the *Ādi Granth*. It is probable that neither of these books was composed till at least fifty years after the death of Kabir, and they can hardly be regarded as retaining in all passages the actual words of the teacher, much less such words without additions:

I neither touched ink nor paper, nor did I take a pen into my hand; to the sages of all four ages Kabīr declared his word by mouth.

Though it is inadvisable to express any definite opinion on such a subject, until the contents of the *Bijak* have been carefully examined and compared with the productions of a later age, yet there is reason to believe that the teaching of Kabīr has gradually become more and more Hindu in form. At any rate we have no right to assume that the teaching of Kabir was identical with that given at the present time by the Mahants of the Panth that bears his name.

So far the contents of the Bijak have only been made known in part, and all who have studied the book allow that it contains many passages that are practically unintelligible to us of a later age, dark riddles which they are unable to interpret. An expositon of teaching which is based upon a selection from selections, must of necessity be defective; and may possibly be misleading, if regarded as an interpretation of the whole. A mind influenced by Christian thought is naturally inclined to dwell upon teaching that seems to have affinity with truths that it is in a position to appreciate passages which to the original teacher may have seemed to less important are hurriedly passed over because the reader through lack of knowledge is unable to estimate their value.

Bearing in mind these limitations we will proceed to examine the teaching of Kabīr as illustrated by quotations from the *Bijak* and the *Ādi Granth*.[1] We shall meet with teaching which will immediately call to mind passages of Scripture;[2] we shall meet with condemnations of falsehood which as regards directness of speech, should amply satisfy the feelings of the most militant type of Missionary. We shall admire the Teacher, alike for his sincerity and his courage.

The World and Religion

There are men who live in the world as though it were their permanent abode; men who take thought for the body and pay heed to its desires, as though it were a permanent possession; men who accumulate riches as though they were free from the thraldom

---

[1] See *The Bijak*, p. 732

[2] To those who have a knowledge of the subject the references to Sūfi teaching will probably appear to be very numerous.

of death. Such men will never obtain true happiness, nor will they unravel the knots by which they are bound, until they look to God for help. He who would know God must die to the world. God is a jealous God who loves not those who entertain in their hearts love for another God. Man cannot serve God and mammon. Only those who give their entire heart to God will realise their true self. The knowledge of God is as a precious diamond, recognised only by those who are spiritually minded. The true servants of God are few in number, and to the worldly minded seem as men who are beside themselves.

All who live in this world are liable to temptation; the black snake coils itself round the sandal tree. The poison of the snake received into the body works corruption and issues in death. Those alone escape who place their trust in God.

Selfishness and pride of intellect are the enemies of spiritual development.[1] Those only see God who have a forgiving spirit. The struggle against evil is hard to maintain, but slothfulness is fatal. The opportunity lost may not recur. *Now* is the time to prepare for the journey that lies before us.

ILLUSTRATIONS

1. We are idols of clay, to which the name of man is given; we are guests of four days, in a very great pit of fuel is our place. G.[2]

2. The physician has died, the sick man has died, the whole world has died; One, O Kabir, has not died, for whom is no weeper. G.

3. O man, thou hast a precious body indeed. Thy flesh is not used. No ornaments are made of thy bones; no drums are mounted with thy leather. B.

4. Man in this world is wholly sinful from his very birth, and there are many ready to claim his body. The parents say, "He is our child and we have nourished him for our own benefit." The wife says, "He is my husband," and like a tigress wishes to seize him. The children gaze at him, and like the god of death, keep their mouths wide open for support. The vulture and the crow look forward to his death. The pigs and the dogs wait on the road for his

---

[1] Kabīr's condemnation of pride and commendation of humility are much more in accordance with the teaching of Sūfī Saints than with the practice of Hindu pandits.

[2] G indicates a quotation from the *Ādi Granth*; B quotation from the *Bijak*.

bier to pass on its way to the burning ghat. The fire says, "I shall not leave him, until he is utterly consumed." The earth says, 'I shall obtain him.' The wind thinks of carrying him off. O ignorant people, you speak of this body as your house; do you not see that a hundred enemies hang about your throat. Beguiled by the illusion of this world, you regard such a body as your own. So many desire a share in your body that you will live in trouble all your life. O madmen, you do not wake up to a knowledge of this, but repeatedly say, 'It is mine'. It is mine.' B.

5. Adding kauri to kauri he brings together lakhs and crores.

At the time of departure he gets nothing at all, even his *langoti* is plucked away from him. G.

6. To the miser wealth is given for the sake of keeping it. The fool says, 'The property is mine.'

When the staff of Yama strikes his head, the matter is decided in a moment. G.

7. Immense riches and a kingdom which extends from the rising of the sun unto the going down thereof could not equal the pleasure arising out of devotion (to God). Of what use then is wealth ? B.

8. Fire does not burn it, the wind does not carry it away, no thief comes near it; collect the wealth of the name of Rām, that wealth is never lost. G.

9. For gold he is not obtained, Rām is obtained for the price of the heart. G.

10. Without devotion life is spent to no purpose; without worshipping the Lord in the society of the pious, happiness remains in none. G.

11. The poor soul of man is tied to this world with many knots. It cannot unloose itself without the help of God. B.

12. He (God) whom you seek, is near you. He is always near to his devotees and far from those who do not worship Him. B.

13. Kabīr says, Where shall I find a supremely loving saint who will give pleasure, destroy pain and remove all stains of sin ? B.

14. Who whilst living, goes on dying, he lives again; in this wise he is absorbed in space; he who remains in the darkness, unaffected by the darkness, is no more thrown into the sea of existence. G.

15. Now my mind on the contrary has become eternal; then the mind is known, when one dies when living. G.

16. At the bank of a river and at a Tīrtha there is no reassurance for the mind of him who is clinging to light ways. G.

17. What is muttering, what austerity, what vows and worship to him in whose heart there is another love ? G.

18. What is muttering, what austerity and control of the passions, what vows and ablutions; so long as the right, loving worship of the Lord is not known ? G.

19. In the heart there is a looking-glass, the face is not seen in it; then only you will see the face when the doubleness of the heart is removed. B.

20. The pure diamond is sold for plates of gold. He who knows not its value, what will he do with it ? B.

21. The diamond was lying on the road, besmeared with ashes: many in their ignorance passed it by, but the diamond specialist picked it up. B.

22. Pearls are scattered on the road; the blind draw near and depart; without the light of the Lord, the world passes them by. G.

23. The black snake is in the heart. It has deposited venom in the souls of all; the few who sincerely worship the true God, will be saved. B.

24. Why should one suffer a dog to listen to the *Smritis* ; why should one sing the praises of Hari in the presence of a *Sakat*? that Rām, Rām is contained in all should on no account be told to a *Sakat* ; why should one suffer a crow to feed on camphor ? why should one give a black snake milk to drink ? the instruction of the foolish is waste of knowledge; a maund of soap cannot wash charcoal white. G.

25. Sandal, restrain thy fragrance, on thy account the wood is cut down; the living slay the living and regard only the dead. B.

26. He is naturally called drunk, who is drinking the juice of Rām and meditating on Divine knowledge. G.

27. If one take nectar and besprinkle a *nīm* tree, its nature does not leave it, says Kabīr. G.

28. Venomous snakes have twined round the sandal tree. What can the sandal do ? in every pore venom has soaked in, where shall nectar enter ? B.

29. The snake of separation has attached itself to the body, and darted its fangs into the heart. Into the body of the Sādhu it finds no admission : prepare yourself for what may happen. B.

30. In the small pond, O fish, the net is spread by the fisherman; in this small pond thou will not escape, think again of the ocean. G.

31. The pride of intellect is manifold, now a swindler, now a

thief; now a liar, now a murderer; men, sages and gods have run after it in vain; its mansion has a hundred gates. B.

32. In pride there is adversity, in sin there is suffering; in kindness there is stability, and in forgiveness there is God. B.

33. Unless you have a forgiving spirit, you will not see God. You may speechify as much as you like, but without a forgiving nature you will never reach Him. B.

34. He who enters into intimacy with the highest light, he subdues the five senses. Religious merit and demerit, both he discards. G.

35. What thou art doing tomorrow, do now; what thou art doing now, do at once: afterwards nothing will be done, when death comes on thy head. G.

36. Now is the time to prepare, henceforth the path is difficult; the travellers all hasten to purchase, where there is neither trade nor market. B.

37. The righteous man does not give up his piety, though he meet with crores of wicked persons: even as the sandal tree is not deprived of its cooling properties though venomous snakes twine round it. B.

38. With the *Sakat* company should not be kept, one should flee far from him; if a black vessel is touched, some stain is received. G.

RELIGION IN LIFE

God is one; how has it come about that there are many religions? All men are of one blood; how comes it about that they are separated by religion and by caste? God is one: the Hindus are therefore at fault in their worship of many gods. These are in truth the creation of Māyā; they have their origin in sin and are themselves the cause of sin in others.

Muhammadans put their trust in circumcision, Hindus adore the *Vedas* and the beauties of Nature. The things which are seen are transitory. True worship should have as its object the unseen source of all truth, the unseen Creator of the universe.

The Hindus bathe in sacred streams, go on pilgrimage to sacred places, bow down to images of brass and stone, and think that in so doing they are honouring God. In this they are mistaken. What God desires is purity of heart; to rest in symbols that should lead men on to God is to be guilty of idolatry.

Hindūs and Muhammadans alike profess to fast, but curb not the desires of the flesh; they praise God with their lips, but their hearts are far from Him. All such religion is vain.

Muhammadans repeat prayers and texts of scripture which they cannot understand; Hindūs believe in gods who destroy men, sport with milkmaids and assume the form of animals. All such religion is vain.

Vain too are the distinctions of caste. All shades of colour are but broken arcs of light, all varieties in human nature are but fragments of true humanity. The right to approach God is not the monopoly of Brahmins but is freely granted to all who are characterised by sincerity of heart. He who reflects on Brahm is rightly called a Brahmin. The distinctions observed by Hindus are merely productive of that pride which God abhors. The rules regarding impurity deal merely with externals and cleanse not the thoughts of the heart.

Hindus believe in transmigration. If they would be free from the trials of this world, let them meditate on the Supreme and attend the courts of His temple.

Above all things let men speak and practise the truth. Suffer all men to worship God according to their convictions. Be not the slaves of tradition and love not controversy for its own sake. Fear not to walk upon unbeaten tracks, if such tracks bring you near to Him who is the truth.

Men are saved by faith and not by works. None can understand the mind of God; put your trust in Him; let Him do what seemeth Him good. Spiritual joy is felt, though it cannot be expressed in words, To set forth the glory of God is a task beyond the powers of human language. Those who put their trust in God are no longer subject to fear. Perfect love casteth out fear.

ILLUSTRATIONS

39. God, light, sound and one woman, from these have sprung Harī, Brahma and Tripurāri. Innumerable are emblems of Shiva and Bhavānī, which they have established, but they know not their own beginning nor end. A dwelling has been prepared for them: Hari, Brahmā and Shiva are the three headmen and each has his own village. B.

40. I and you are of one blood, and one life animates us both;

from one mother is the world born; what knowledge is this which makes us separate ? B.

41. All have come from the same country and have landed at one ghat, but the evil influences of this world have divided us into innumerable sects. B.

42. From whence have Hindus and Turks come ? By whom have these ways been started ? Having searched and reflected in thy mind tell me. By whom have Paradise and Hell been made ? G.

43. By force and love circumcision is made : I shall not agree to it, O brother. If God will make me a Turk by him will I be circumcised : If a man becomes a Turk by being circumcised, what shall be done with a woman ? She must remain a Hindu. G.

44. If your *Khudā* wished circumcision, he would have sent you circumcised into the world, If by circumcision you become a Muhammadan in that case what should you do with your women. A women is said to be the half of man; being so, would she remain a Hindu ? If by wearing the sacred thread a man becomes a Brahmin then what do your women wear ? They by birth are Shudrins, why should you being a *Pānde* take the meal placed by them before you ? Whence have the Hindus and Muhammadans come ? Who has started these religious systems. Think well in your hearts who has obtained heaven. O mad man, give up the illusion of this world. O brethren, you resist (the warnings of conscience). Kabīr is on the road to God and is marching on to his end, forsaking all partial views. B.

45. Is Brahma great, or he by whom he is produced ? Is the *Veda* great or he from whom it is come ? G.

46. What thou seest, that is passing away : whom thou dost not see, on him continue to reflect. When in the tenth gate the key is given : then the sight of the merciful one is obtained. G.

47. A well-made picture is of high value : leave the picture and think of the painter. B.

Variously coloured is this immense world : leaving the picture, keep the painter in thy thoughts. G.

48. O Saints, the world has gone mad; if I tell the truth it comes down upon me to kill me, but believes a lie. I have seen the devout and the pious who regularly bathe in the mornings. They forsake God and worship stones; in them there is no wisdom . . . . They have commenced to worship brass and stones and are proud of their pilgrimages. They wear garlands, caps and frontal marks

and chhaps on their arms, and engage in singing the praises of their gods; they have forsaken God." B.

49. The beads are of wood, the gods of stone, the Ganges and the Jumna are water. Rāma and Krishna are dead. The four *Vedas* are fictitious stories. B.

50. If by worshipping stones one can find God, I shall worship a mountain ; better than these stones (idols) are the stones of the flour mill with which men grind their corn. B.

51. Although I entreat much, even falling at their feet, with tears in my eyes, the Hindus do not forsake idol-worship and the Muhammadans are too stiff-necked to hear anything. B.

52. For the sake of bathing, there are many Tirthās, O foolish mind; for the sake of worshipping there are many idols. Kabīr says, No emancipation is thus obtained, emancipation is in the service of Hari. G.

53. If by immersion in the water salvation be obtained, the frogs bathe continually. As the frogs, so are these men, again and again they fall into the womb. G.

54. A stone is shaped by the hammer and formed into an image, with breasts and feet; If this image be true, then it will eat the hammerer. G.

55. Kabīr says, I am completely at a loss; is the Tīrtha great or the servant of Hari ? G.

56. As long as the sun does not rise the stars sparkle; so as long as perfect knowledge (of God) is not obtained men practice ritualism. B.

57. The water is near but the cattle do not drink in wading through it. By continually remembering Hari water issues. That water is pure, says Kabīr. G.

58. Within his heart is filthiness; though he bathe at a Tīrtha, he will not go to Paradise. By the belief of the people nothing is effected, Rām is not ignorant. G.

59. The Hindus fast on the 11th of the light half of each month for singhārā (a sort of fruit) and milk. They give up food during the day, but do not curb the evil passions of their heart and take meat. The Muhammadans keep fasts, repeat the *namār* and (early in the morning) cry aloud Bismillāh like the crowing of a cock .... Kabīr says, "O saints do not call on Rāma or Khudā" B.

60. O Moulvi, what books are you explaining ? Although day and night you remain babbling and jabbering you have not found

out the one (true) religion. B.

61. All have exclaimed, Master, Master, but to me this doubt arises; How can they sit down with the Master, whom they do not know ? G.

62. The mind knows everything and knowingly commits vices; what is the good of the lamp, if with it in his hand a man falls into the well ? G.

63. Follow the true Sāhib (God) who will uphold you in all your trials. He was not born in Dasrath's family and did not oppress the king of Lankā. Jasodā did not fondle him in her lap and he did not enter the womb of Devakī. He did not ravage the world. He did not descend into *Pātāl* to deceive Bali. He did not fight with King Bali nor did he kill Hiranyaksh, throwing him down on the ground. He did not assume the form of a boar nor did he destroy the Kshattriyas. He did not hold the Gobar Dhana on the tip of his finger nor did he remain in the jungle with the milk-maids (of Muttra and Brindaban). He is neither *shalagrāma*, nor any other stone; he is not fish, nor tortoise, dwellers in the water. He died not at Dwarawati nor was his corpse buried at Jagannāth. Kabīr proclaims, let none follow such teaching; he whom they believe to be of gross and material elements is of subtle principles. B.

64. Brahmā is dead with Shiva who lived in Kāshi; the immortals are dead. In Mathura Krishna, the milkman, died. The ten incarnations are dead. Machhindra Nāth, Gorakh, Dattātreya and Vyās are no longer living. Kabīr says, with a loud voice; "All these persons have fallen into the slip-knot of death." B.

65. Whilst dwelling in the womb, there is no clan nor caste; from the seed of Brahm the whole creation is made.

Say, O Pandit. When were the Brahmins made; by saying, "I am a Brahmin," thy life and religion are lost.

If thou art a Brahmin born of a Brahmin woman; why hast thou not come in another way ?

Whose art thou, the Brahmin ? Whose am I, the Sūdra; whose blood am I ? Whose milk art thou ?

Kabīr says, who reflects on Brahm, he by me is called a Brahmin. G.

66. Colour proceeds from colour, yet behold all are but one; of what colour then is life ? Think well of this. G.

67. By the touch of others you Brahmins consider yourselves

polluted. Let me ask you, who is lower than you ? You are puffed
up with pride. Great pride never produces any good. How will he
who is called the vanquisher of the proud bear with your pride ?

68. There is impurity in water, impurity in earth; there is impurity at the time of birth, there is impurity in the hour of death,
there is impurity in destruction (corruption of the body) ?

In the eyes is impurity, in the speech is impurity and in the ears
impurity.

In rising and sitting impurity clings to man, impurity falls into
the food.

The way of ensnaring every one knows, but few only the way of
escape.

Kabīr says, those who reflect in their heart on Rām, in them no
impurity is found. G.

69. As fixed and movable things, as worms and moths, in many
and various ways have we been born.

Many such houses will be inhabited by us, till at length we
return to the womb of Rām. G.

70. Having wandered through the 84 lakhs of wombs he has
come into the world; now having gone out of the body he has no
spot nor place. G.

71. Kabīr says, Meditate thou on the Supreme, Go to his house,
that thou come not again. G.

72. Clear away the pain of birth and death, the pleasure of
works, that the soul may be liberated from rebirth. G.

73. To be truthful is best of all, if the heart be truthful. A man
may speak as much as he likes: but there is no pleasure apart from
truthfulness. B.

74. He who has no cheek upon his tongue, no truth in his heart:
with such a one keep not company. He will kill you on the high-
way. B.

75. No act of devotion can equal truth; no crime is so heinous
as falsehood; in the heart where truth abides, there is my abode.
G.

76. If you are a true dealer, open the market of veracity; keep
clean yonr inward man, and repel oppression to a distance. G.

77. Put a check upon the tongue, speak not much; associate with
the wise; investigate the words of the teacher. G.

78. Let truth be your rate of interest, and fix it in your heart;
a real diamond should be purchased; the mock gem is waste of

capital. G.

79. I have examined the religious doctrines of Muhammadans and Hindus. They do not lay aside their bigotry for the sake of relish for their tongues. B.

80. Kabīr cries aloud to his fellows, "Ascend the sandal ridge: whether there be a road prepared or not, what matters it to me ?" G.

81. O God, thou knowest thine own movements, I have no power to know them. Kabīr says, "In this the world has erred and has been led into doubt." B.

82. Thy name is my support, as the flower will grow out of the lotus stalk. Kabīr says, 'I am the slave of thy house, vivify or kill me, as it pleases thee. G.

83. As many as are making efforts, they are drowned; the ocean is not crossed by them.

Though they be performing works, and many abstinences, their mind is burnt by egotism. G.

84. Kabīr says, I am a sacrifice to my own Guru, by whom I remain in connexion with the society of the pious. G.

85. O Mādhva, my thirst for water does not cease; in drinking the water the fire increases still more.

Thou art the ocean, I am the fish of the water; I dwell in the water; without the water, I am done for. G.

86. In me there is nothing mine; whatever there is, that is thine, In entrusting what is thine to thee, what remains mine ? G.

87. If a dumb person eats molasses, what can he say about it when questioned ? G.

88. If I make the seven oceans ink, if I make the trees my pen, if I make the earth the paper, the glory of Hari cannot be written ? G.

89. If fear of God springs up, fear goes; then fear is absorbed in the fear of God.

If the fear of God subsides, then fear again cleaves to man; when a man loses the fear of God, fear springs up in his heart: he dies. G.

90. Where the fearless one is, there is no fear, where fear is, there Harī is not; Kabīr says, having reflected in his mind; "Hear this, O ye saints." G.

91. On the day on which I died, on that day joy sprang up. The Lord met with me, Govind honours his own companion. G.

92. Death of which the world is afraid, is joy to my mind; by

death the full perfect joy is obtained. G.

THE WAY TO GOD

Kabīr was a great believer in quiet reflection as a means of approach to God.

He recognised that the ancient scriptures of both Mohammadans and Hindūs were of a certain value, but felt that their value had been greatly overestimated.

Through the understanding of the heart and mind man becomes conscious of God's existence. Thoughts and feelings are expressed in words, words are composed of letters. All that is of use in communicating to man a knowledge of God has a significance that may well be regarded as sacred. What is multiform now will hereafter be seen to be single. The 52 letters[1] will give place to the one letter which denotes man's union with God. The revelation of God, given in Rām, surpasses all other revelations in simplicity and purity, but the unity of Truth has not as yet been fully apprehended.

Through his own powers man cannot attain to a knowledge of God; but God will reveal Himself to those who listen to his voice. He alone overcomes doubts and truly lives who has welcomed this message in his heart.

Strange and sad it seems to those who have experienced a knowledge of the Truth that men should be content to grope on still in darkness.

Men are not equally endowed with spiritual insight. The mass of men must seek guidance of those who have, through a knowledge of God, discovered for themselves the way. The Hindus trust in vain to those who wear the symbol of sacrifice while they lead lives of pride and self-indulgence. Helmsmen of this kind will never bring the boat to the haven where it should be. Others there are who practise all kinds of austerities, but mistaking the means for the end find not the true path. Those who escape not themselves from death, are unable to impart to others the gift of life.

The true guide is one whose love is fixed on God; who recognises his own worthlessness apart from God; who lives for others and

---

[5] Kabīr probably reckoned that there were 52 consonants in Sanskrit and Arabic, the sacred languages of Hindus and Muhammadans.

godlike himself has entered into life. For such a one death has lost its terrors. He is the true ascetic and walks in the path of life.

ILLUSTRATIONS

93. O Qāzi, What book is expounded by thee; all such as are pondering on the book are killed; no one has obtained true knowledge; give up the book, adore, Rām, O foolish one; thou art practising heavy oppression. Kabīr puts his trust on Rām; the Turks are consumed and defeated.

94. Thou expoundest the book right that Allah is no woman or man; but by reading and perusing nothing is effected; when there is no information in the heart. G.

95. By the Turk God is known from worship, by the Hindu from the *Veda* and *Puranas*; in order to form the mind divine knowledge should be read to some extent. G.

96. Thou shouldst ride on thy own reflection; thou shouldst put thy foot into the stirrup of tranquility of mind. Kabīr says, Those are good riders who keep aloof from the *Veda* and *Qoran*. G.

97. I know that reading is good, but better than reading is meditation; the attachment to Rām I do not give up, though people revile me. G.

98. The 52 letters are joined together by me, but I am not able to know one letter; Kabīr tells the word of the true one! who becomes a Pandit, he remains fearless.

The profession of the Pandit is for the sake of the people, he who is killed in divine knowledge, he reflects the truth. In whose heart such an understanding is; he will know it, says Kabīr. G.

99. Remove doubt, put aside the paper; having investigated the 52 letters apply thy mind to the feet of Hari. G.

100. As the stars at down pass away, so the world passes away; these two letters (Rām) do not pass away, them Kabīr has seized. G.

101. There are many words and there is a great difference between them: accept the true word. Kabīr says he who has found the true word, has no pleasure in this life. B.

102. My word is of the word; hear it, go not astray; if man wishes to know the truth, let him investigate the word. G.

103. By the power of the word the sin of this world is destroyed. The word makes kings forsake their kingdoms. He who has investi-

gated the word has done his work well. B.

104. Without hearing the word it is utter darkness; say, whither shall anyone go; without finding the gateway of the word, man will ever be astray. G.

105. Without the word the Shāstrās are blind. Say whither shall one go? They do not find the gateway of the word but grope on still in darkness. B.

106. There are many words, but take the pith of them; he who takes not the essence, says Kabīr, will live a profitless life. G.

107. Doubt has triumphed over the whole world. No one has overcome it. He who finds out the word will overcome it. B.

108. Think whence the world has come and where has it established itself. Kabīr says, I am a lover of the word which has shown me the unseen (God). B.

109. I have wept for this world but no one has wept with me; he alone will weep with me who understood the word. B.

110. All speak of God, but to me this doubt arises, how can they sit down with God whom they do not know? B.

111. Thou pasturest us, never bringing us to the other side; Thou art a Brahmin, I am a weaver [of Kāshi, understand my divine knowledge. Thou petitionest Kings and Rājās, my meditation is with Hari. G.

112. The jogis, ascetics, austere devotees and Sānyāsis wander about at many tirthas; those with plucked out hair, those with munj cord, the silent ones, those who are wearing plaited hair, all are dying at the end; the Tantras are attended to by them, but not Rām; on whose tongue is put the name of Rām. What can Yama do to him? The *Shāstras*, *Vedas*, astrology and many, many grammars they know: they know the Tantras, Mantras and all medicines, yet at the end they must die; they enjoy dominion, an umbrella and many beautiful women; betel, camphor, perfume and sandal, yet at the end they must die; all the *Vedas*, *Purāṇas* and *Smritis* are searched by them but in no wise are they spared; Kabīr says, Utter Rām, he extinguishes birth and death. G.

113. "The Pundits are in error by reading the *Vedas*. They have no common sense. They daily go through their morning and evening rites and other ceremonies with great punctuality and regularity. They have caused the Gāyatri to be read and repeated in the four yugs; ask them who has obtained freedom from sin by doing so?

They consider themselves polluted by the touch or others: ask them who is lower then thay are?" B.

114. Who wear dhotīs of three yards and a half and three fold cords; on whose necks are rosaries, and whose hands are white lotus; these cheats of Benares are not called the Saints of Hari. Having scoured the vessels they put them on, having washed the wood they light it; digging out the earth they make two fire places, but eat whole men. G.

115. If by wandering about naked union with Hari be obtained; then every deer of the forest will become emancipated.

What are the naked? What are those with skins? When they do not know the Supreme?

If by shaving the head, perfection is obtained; the sheep is emancipated, no one is lost.

Kabīr says, Hear, O man and brother; without the name of Rām no one has obtained salvation. G.

116. In our house the string of the body is continually stretched out; on thy breast is a sacrificial thread; Thou readest the *Veda* and *Gyatri*; in our heart dwells Govind.

On my tongue is Viṣṇu, in my eyes Nārāyan, in my heart dwells Govind; when at the gate of Yama he will ask thee, O fool, What wilt thou say to Mukand?

We are the cattle, thou art the cowherd, O Lord, who art our keeper through the several births.

117. What can he do whose teacher is blind? The blind pushes the blind and both fall into a well. B.

118. How is it possible to reach the city when the guide cannot point out the road; when the boat is crazy, how shall the passengers get clear of the ghat? G.

119. The man who fixes his love on the true teacher is contained in him. They could not be separated they have two bodies but one spirit. B.

120. I am the worst of all, every one is good except me; who considers himself in this light, he is my friend. G.

121. The tree bears not fruit for itself, nor for itself does the stream collect its waters; for the benefit of others alone does the sādhu assume a bodily shape. G.

122. The body is wounded by a spear; the head is broken off and left in the flesh; it cannot be extracted without the loadstone; a thousand other stones are of no avail. G.

123. From heaven and hell I am freed by the favour of the true Gurū; I remain in the wave of the lotus foot at the end and the beginning. G.

124. In this society thou wilt not die; if thou knowest his order, thou wilt be united with the Lord. G.

125. Death, by which the whole world is frightened; that death is lighted up by the word of the Guru. G.

126. Making divine knowledge and meditation his patched quilt, and the word the needle, he puts the thread into the head of the needle; making the five elements his deer-skin he walks in the way of the Guru. G.

The *Bījak*

The *Bījak* (account book or invoice) is recognised as the authoritative exposition of Kabīr's teaching. It was probably produced about 1570, or some 20 years before the teaching of Nānak was embodied in the *Ādi Granth* by Guru Arjun, the fifth Guru of the Sikh community. Most of the sayings attributed to Kabīr in the *Ādi Granth* are also to be found in the *Bījak*, though the editor of the *Granth* has not scrupled to re-arrange the subject matter.

There are several printed editions of the *Bījak*. The two best known editions are both supplied with a commentary, the one by Mahārājah Bishwa Nāth Singh of Rewah[1] and the other by Bābā Puran Dass. The former edition has been printed at Benares, Lucknow and Bombay, and also without the commentary at Gayā; the latter at Lucknow and Allahabad (1905). Of the former it is said that "the editor has tried to expound the *Saguṇa Upāsanā* of Rāma through the teaching of Kabīr, where by the term *Saguṇa Upāsanā* is meant the religious contemplation of Rāma as the embodiment

---

[1] In the life of Kabīr by Munshi Mohan Lall Kayasth of Lucknow, a work which is largely based upon *Anurag Sagar*, it is stated that Kabīr visited Turkistan and on his return spent sometime with the Mahārājah of Rewah by whom he was most hospitably received. In return for kindness received Kabīr promised the Mahārājah who at the time was childless that his descendants should sit upon his throne for 42 generations.

of all good qualities." This edition is not well thought of by Kabīr Panthis. The author of the second commentary, Bābā Pūran Dāss, lived at Nagjhari, in the district of Burhanpur, Gujarat, and flourished about 1837.

The Rev. Prem Chand of the Baptist Mission, Monghyr, had another edition printed in Calcutta in 1890. The editor of this edition writes :

"Some thirty year ago I was lent a manuscript copy of the *Bījak*, taken from the Murshidabad edition. This I had copied out and afterwards compared my copy with others from different parts of the country. I found in these a certain number of *Dohas* (couplets) which were not in my copy and these I had printed at the end of the book. The other poetical pieces were the same in all editions. I corrected various clerical errors and separated words which had been allowed to run into one another and added a few footnotes to make the meaning clear to any ordinary Hindi scholar."

This edition contains 83 *Ramaini,* 113 *Shabda,* 33 hymns of various kinds and 364 *Sākhis.* To these have been added 60 *Sākhis* found in other editions.

The Rev. Ahmad Shāh in the translation of the *Bījak* that he has now in hand will probably throw additional light on literary problems connected with this book.

THE DOCTRINE OF SHABDA (WORD)

A doctrine which might be so described is taught in many of the Hindu religious sects, but it is not easy to determine in each particular case either the origin or character of this teaching.

In the writings of Kabīr three thoughts seem to underlie such teaching (1) All thought is expressed in language, (2) Every letter of the alphabet, as a constituent part of language, has significance, and (3) The plurality of letters and words now in use will appear as one, when the Māyā that deludes men in their present condition shall have been overcome. The two-lettered Rām seems to Kabīr the nearest approach in this world to the unity of Truth or the letterless one.

A distinguished Sanskrit scholar explained to me the Hindū conception of Shabda somewhat in this way. Man desires knowledge. Knowledge is obtainable by meeans of (1) Perception and (2) Inference. These two channels are acknowledged by all and to them are added by some (3) *Shabda,* sound (including the voice of the teacher?) and (4) *Uparnam* or reasoning by analogy.

By Mimānsists all verbal information is regarded as authoritative in itself, unless it can be shown to be derived from a corrupt source. Those who deny that the Vedas are eternal or self-derived should prove that the source from which they are derived is tainted. The Mīmānsists do not believe in a personal God but there are others who accept this teaching and also believe in the personality of God. Such regard the *Vedas* as a God-given revelation.

The term *Shabda* does not occur in the *Vedas,* but in one Hymn *Vāk* (Speech) is personified.

For further information this scholar referred me to the third volume of John Muir's *Original Sanskrit Texts,* which deals with the *Vedas,* their origin, inspiration and authority.

It is not improbable that this doctrine, as set forth in the literature of the Kabīr Panth has been influenced by the writings of St. John, as is confessedly the case as regards the teaching of the Rādhā-swāmi Sect of modern origin. In the Hindi translation of the *New testament* Logos (Word) is represented by *Bachan* and not by *Shabda.*

CHAPTER 4

Sākhis Attributed to Kabīr

ALL Kabīr Panthis have at their command a considerable number of *Sākhis* or rhyming couplets, bearing witness to the truth.[1] The rhythm of many of these is very fine, with the result that important teaching given in this form is easily remembered.

It is not at all likely that all the *Sākhis* attributed to Kabīr were really uttered by him, but most of them are in substance consistent with teaching to be met with in the *Bijak*. A good linguist would probably, on linguistic grounds, reject many as of later origin,[2]

Many of the *Sākhis* embody teaching such as was current among Sufis and embodied in Persian poetry. Some suggest verses of the Bible or Qorān, some in slightly different form have been attributed to other authors and may be regarded as expressing truths generally current in the country. We may safely credit Kabīr with a considerable amount of originality and; even where originality seems unlikely, feel grateful to him for the genius with which he has given expression to old thoughts.[3]

In making this selection I have been guided by the judgement of Kabīr Panthis and also by own judgement as regards the subject matter and the rhythm of the original. I have allowed a certain number of *Sākhis* to retain their place in this collection in spite of the fact that they have been previously quoted.

1. My Lord's a store supplier great, in merchandise he deals; nor beams nor scales, in his own hands this great world weighs and feels.
                                                                            —*Fallon*

[1]*Sakhi* is the corruption of a Sanskrit word meaning evidence.

[2]For the benefit of Hindi scholars this collection of Sakhis has also been printed in the original Hindi. A collection of 2,500 Kabīr *Sākhis* has been published at the Advocate Press, Lucknow.

[3]It has seemed best to omit all reference to possible sources, until so complicated a subject has been more thoroughly investigated.

Shāms Tabrez, the famous Sūfi, wrote :

Who is that person who weighs and distributes without scales or measure, yet his measuring and distribution is correct ?

2. He who made the whole world, that Guru was manifested; the Guru who saw him with his eyes, that Guru revealed Him to men. Cf 1 Jn. i 3·1.

3. One poor spirit bound with many ties; in its own strength it cannot escape, till God rescue it.

Piw, the word translated God, is a term applied to husband by wife; the loved one.

4. The chelā whose Guru is blind, while he himself is more blind; the blind one gives a push to his blind fellow; they both fall into the well.

Neither understands the truth; one pushes this way, the other another; both come to grief.

5. The soul (*ātmā*) and the great soul (*paramātmā*) for many ages remained apart; the Gurū came as a dealer (*dallāl*) and made of them a beateous mixture.

6. A sinner from my birth, in sin from head to foot I lie; O generous giver, comforter, but listen to my cry.   — *Fallon*

With the reading in the ordinary Hindi text, translate second line, "O God, remover of pain, deliver me".

A Guru should be as a knife grinder; the rust of a life time he removes in a moment.

7. Regard your Guru as a knife grinder, let him grind your heart; cleansing the heart from all impurity, let him make it bright as a mirror.

8. Kāl hovers over the head, Kāl comes not into sight; Kabīr says, Lay hold of the Gurus words (the *mantra*) that he may rescue your soul from death.

9. The Guru is the potter and the disciple the vessel; he removes all defects. He places the support (*Sahārā*) within before with blows he fashions the vessel into shape.

The *Hahārā* or *Sahārā* is an instrument of wood or stone which with one hand the potter holds within the jar while with the other he strikes. In this way the wall of the jar is able to resist the force of the blows administered by the other hand from without. The public may be deceived into thinking that the Guru is cruel in his treatment of the chelā. See picture of Potter.

10. As he removes his rosary, life passes away and he knows not

A Potter at work, to illustrate Sakhi (9).   *(to face p. 47)*

the secrets of his heart; throw away the rosary of the hand and revolve the rosary of the heart.

There is a double play upon words : *Man*=heart, *manka*= rosary; *Pher* = secrets, also *Pher* = revolve.

11. A man steals an anvil, and offers a needle as alms; he climbs aloft to see how distant is the chariot.

The man who makes this miserable offering thinks that God will be so pleased with his generosity that he will at once send a chariot to fetch him to heaven.

Fallon translates thus :

He steals an anvil and a needle gives in charity; he then the house top mounts to see how far's heaven's chariot sent for me.

12. Apart from life, life comes not into existence, life lives on life; refuse not to have pity on life; Pandit, take thought on this.

13. Under the influence of Shabda one man died to the world, another gave up his throne; those who have understood Shabda, their work is completed.

14. A man may be a great preacher, as the vulture soars in the sky; but its food is on the earth; does flying in the air make of it a saint ?

Preaching in itself is useless, unless the life corresponds. The vulture may fly in the sky, but on the earth it devours refuse and so can never be respected.

15. Whatever I have is not my own it is thine; it is thine own that I give thee; what have I ?

16. Strain your water before you drink it; test your Guru before you commit yourself to him.

17. The humble obtain salvation to a man, so many as are sub-missive; those sink who are puffed up with the pride of high birth.

The reference here is to the ocean of rebirths; the humble-minded reach the further shore in safety; the proud sink in the waters and escape not from the troubles of this world.

18. When the Guru is covetous, his disciple will be grasping; both employ trickery; both will be drowned in their folly, having boarded a ship of stone.

The chelā to protect himself from the greed of the Guru conceals the extent of his possessions. At first he was tricked into owning that he had property, but not a second time; he tricked the guru. In this way both fail to cross the ocean of rebirths. In one of the Kabīr legends, it is said that Kabīr was placed on board a boat

loaded with stones that it might sink in mid stream, but he miraculously escaped. The idea may have been suggested by this *sākhī*.

19. From one country have they come; at one *ghāt* have they
disembarked. They have breathed the air of the world, and on
twelve paths have they gone their way.

Bārah bāt is a proverbial expression, scattered, dispersed, cast to
the winds. All men are of one blood, all are born of human parentage, caste distinctions, invented of men, are productive of much
evil. Fallon translates :

All from one country come, alighted also at one port; by winds
of worldly passion driven, all scattered are in sport.

20. The lascivious, the ill-tempered and the covetous, for such
devotion to God is impossible. Brave is the man who for devotion to God is ready to give up caste and family.

21. Small is the door of devotion (*Bhakti*), as the tenth part of
a mustard seed. The heart of man is swollen with pride to the size
of an elephant, how can he pass within ? Cf St. Matt. xix. 24.

22. The great having attained greatness become exceeding proud.
Those who have no knowledge of the true Guru, whatever their
caste, are *chamārs*.

Rom rom the hairs on the human body; there is no spot where
there is no hair, no point at which the great do not display pride.

23. The worship of a devotee and the water of a torrent in the
rains, both flow deep; but that only should be called a river which
continues to flow in the hot weather (Jeth-June).

The devotee whose devotion depends upon prosperity is no true
devotee.

24. He who sows for you thorns, for him do you sow flowers;
you will have flowers at the time of flowering; he will find a *trisūl*.

Trisūl may signify a large thorn or it may mean that such a one
will be punished by Shiva.

25. Do not oppress the weak, their sighs have great power; by
the puffs of the bellows iron is converted to flames (*or* is utterly
consumed).

If the puffs from the skin of a dead animal can do so much, how
much more will the sighs of the living effect. The skin of goats,
buffaloes and bullocks are used as bellows.

26. Be true to God and loving to his servants whether your hair
be long or entirely removed.

Many Bairāgis shaved their heads. To Kabīr such matters were of trivial importance.

27. The *ghāt* in which love dwells not, know that *ghāt* to be a burning *ghāt* (masān); that heart is as the blacksmith's bellows which breathe, but have no life.

There is here a play upon the word *ghāt*. *Ghāt* which=a vessel, is often used of the human heart. *Ghāt*, is also used, as=*ghāt*, the burning *ghāt* where the bodies of the dead are burnt.

28. Love grows not in the fields nor is it on sale in the bazar; the man devoid of love will be bound and cast into hell. (*Yāmpūr*, the city of Yām).

29. He may drink the cup of love who gives his all (lit. his head) to God; the covetous cannot give all, but only know the name of love, *or* He drinks the cup of love who lays down his life for others; he who works for reward, merely speaks of love.

30. A man may read many books before he dies and yet not be a Pandit; he is a Pandit who understands the two and a half letters which form the word Love.

31. There is no work of merit equal to truth and no sin equal to falsehood; in whose heart Truth dwells, in his heart dwells God himself.

32. Those who say and do not are great liars; in the end, when God holds his Durbār, they will be thrust out.

Dhakka khānā is a phrase applied to badmāshes, thrust out of all respectable society.

33. When the sun rises, darkness disappears; before the wisdom of the Guru the corrupt thoughts of men disappear; covetousness destroys sound judgement and pride devotion to God.

34. Weeds destroy the crops; the ignorant destroy the assembly; covetousness spoils devotion, as a mixture of earth destroys the value of saffron.

35. Those who sought found, diving down into deep waters; the heron in its helplessness remained sitting upon the bank.

Fallon gives a different version of this *Sākhi* which he translates: Who in deep waters plunged and sought have found; but foolish me sat by the shore, through fear of being drowned. This form of the saying is attributed to Dharm Dāss.

36. All say 'Lord, Lord' (*Sāhib*), but my fear is of a different kind; when I know not God by sight, where can I take my seat or how shall I sit down with a God whom I have not known?

37. The house of God is distant, as is a tall palm; he who climbs

to the top, tastes of heaven; he who falls is ground to pieces.

38. What you would do to-morrow, do to-day; what you would do to-day do at once; in a moment the deluge (*pralaya*) will come, then what time will there be for doing.

Pralaya is used of the destruction with which each of the several ages closes.

39. When I went in search of evil men, none appeared to view; when I searched my own heart, I felt that none were so evil as myself.

40. Full knowledge of God is not attained when the heart has not been united with God; devotion is simply that of imitation, the colour in not fast.

41. A cage with nine doors, in it a bird like air: that it should remain there is the marvel; what wonder if it escape ?

42. In times of trouble men remember God, but not in times of ease; should they remember God in times of ease, would they ever experience trouble ?

43. Live on friendly terms with all, be ready to speak about all; in word agree with all men, but abide in your own abode.

The rhythm of this *Sākhi* is so fine that I cannot refrain from printing it in Roman character :

> Sab se hiliye, sab se miliye, sab ke lijiye naun;
> Hānji, Hānji, sab se kahiye, basiye apne gāun.

This saying is generally interpreted to mean that men should be tolerant of religious beliefs differing from their own, though in no hurry to surrender traditional beliefs.

I has also been rendered thus :

> Associate with all on friendly terms; address every one with respect (give them their full titles); agree with every one in what he says, and you will have a village of your own to live in, i.e. Humour the public and you will soon have them in your power.

44. Upon seeing the mill revolving, Kabīr wept; the grain that falls between the stones can never escape entire.

45. All men speak of the mill, but none make mention of the pin; the grain that abides by the pin, even its hair is not disturbed.

The two stones of the mill are heaven and earth, nearly all who live upon the earth are overcome of evil; the few who escape are those who abide by the pin, i.e. those who call upon God.

46. The Brahmins of this age are objects of ridicule; give not to them alms: they with their families will go to hell, and take with them their employers (i.e. those who give them fees or alms.)

47. The company of the saints will make your burdens light; the company of the evil means quarrelling throughout the eight watches.

This saying is by Fallon attributed to Tulsi Dāss.

48. That day is blessed which causes you to meet a holy man; as you embrace him fervently, sin is driven from the body.

A saying similar to this to be found among the Muhammadan traditions (*Hadīs*).

49. Through association with a Sādhū comes remembrance of God; that hour is recorded to a man's credit in his account with God; all the rest is as valueless as air.

50. The mirror of God is the body of the Sādhū; he who wishes to see, let him see the invisible in him (the Sādhū.)

51. The Sādhū is the river, love is the water; in that place wash your body; Kabīr says, Be clean, in company with the Sādhūs.

As people wash their clothes on the banks of a river, so should they seek purity of heart through associating with Sādhūs.

52. The tree does not store its fruit for its own use, nor the river its water; for the benefit of others has the Sādhū adopted human form.

53. *Yām* roars like a lion, cries aloud Kabīr; were not the Guru merciful, Yām would tear and rend.

54. He who has chosen a bodily Guru and has failed to recognise the true Guru; time after time he rises and sinks, ensnared in the ocean of existence.

A bodily guru is one who is a guru in outward appearance, one merely qualified to give instruction as to ritual, sacrifice, alms etc., and not to give spiritual counsel.

55. The Chela should be willing to give everything to his Guru; the Guru should refuse to take anything from his chelā.

Many gurus frequently visit the houses of their chelās and by noisy demonstrations in which they are assisted by Bairāgīs and curses extort offerings from those who at first declined to give.

56. The true Guru took the arrow of the Shabda and prepared to

shoot; that which he shot with love found its home within the body.

57. You are the wife of one, but have become the prostitute of many; say with whose corpse will you be burnt? for you are the wife of many.

There is one God whom men should love; what will be the fate of those who love false gods?

58. The true Guru is a great money changer, testing the good and the evil; rescuing from the world the good, he takes it under his own protection.

59. As the snake when it sees the man who has received the *mantra*, lowers its hood; so Kāl, awed by the name written on the *pān* leaf, turns his head away.

The second line contains a reference to the consecration of the pān leaf by the Head Mahant. See ch. 6.

60. The Chakwi remains apart from her mate throughout the night, in the early morning they meet; the man who remains apart from God meets him neither by day nor night.

61. He who removes another's head, removes his own; in God's durbār the account will have to be settled.

62. The power that cannot be described, the form that imparts life (the vision of God is life), whoever becomes one with him (as milk with water); that man, says Kabīr to Dharm Dāss, Kāl cannot destroy.

Union with the true God who has neither form nor shape leads on to the development of man's true self over which death has no power.

63. He who reproaches me is my friend; he supplies the soap to wash my dirty linen.

The man who is reproached pays heed to what is said and reforms. A similar saying is attributed to the Sūfī saint, Imām Ghizāli, who used the word 'washerman' instead of 'soap'.

64. Made articles are quickly destroyed and once destroyed are not put right; by an admixture of vinegar milk is curdled and cannot again be turned to milk.

65. For man to assume a body is difficult; it cannot be done twice. The ripe fruit that falls to the ground, cannot again be attached to the tree.

Hindus who believe in transmigration explain this as meaning that many ages will elapse before any particular person will again enter the world as a man.

66. We know not what the quarter of a second may bring and yet we make plans for the morrow; death comes suddenly as the hawk pounces down on the partridge.

67. The gardener comes to the garden and seeing him the buds cry out, "The full-blown flowers are culled to-day, tomorrow our turn will come."

68. The earth said to the potter, why do you trample on me? the day will come when I shall trample on you.

The potter tramples on the earth to make it workable and plastic.

69. All help the strong; no one helps the weak. A breeze gives fresh life to the fire, but extinguishes the candle.

70. What place has the coward on the wrestling ground? when wrestler meets with wrestler then is a real contest.

71. Consider him a wrestler, striving to attain the favour of God, who though crushed to pieces, refuses to give up the struggle.

In the second line reference is made to an instruction often given to a wrestler by his trainer, 'Crush him to pieces'. (*Us ke purze purze dhīlé kar do*).

72. The days of yore are gone; he loved not God (Hari); of what use is remorse, when the birds have eaten all the crops ?

These words are often used of a 'ne'er do well, when on the point of death.

73. The wood that has already been burnt (in the process of con- version into charcoal) that too cries out. "If I go to the blacksmith's forge, 1 shall be burnt a second time."

Sinners die once in this world and a second time in the world to come.

74. Remain apart from the world, as water refuses to mingle with oil; deposit your heart where is neither death nor the dungeons of *kāl.*

75. Who saves his head, loses his head; who severs his head, finds a head; as the wick of a candle gives additional light when trimmed.

The head is regarded as the most precious of human possessions; a man will give his head for a friend.

76. The pearl is found in the oyster, the oyster is in sea; the diver brings him up; with no one else is the power.

There is probably here a play upon words. The word translated

Diver may also mean, One who lives through death, or conquers after a hard struggle.

77. Consider the parable of the sieve; it suffers the flour to pass, but retains the husk; so men let pass what is good and swallow what is useless.

Sār=that which passes through the sieve. *Asār*=that which is retained.

78. Consider the sugar-cane press; the juice flows out, the fragments of cane remain.

His heart is wanting in wisdom who retains thoughts of no value and disregards spiritual mysteries.

79. All Sādhūs are in appearance alike, resembling a field of poppies; some few thinkers are as red flowers, the rest are perfectly white.

It is the white poppy that is cultivated in Indian fields for the production of opium.

80. Holy men will not relinquish holiness, though they associate with crores of unholy men; though snakes may cling to the sandal tree, it will never lose its coolness.

81. Ask not a Sādhū about his caste, but about his knowledge of God; when you are determining the price of a sword, there is no need to consider the sheath.

The sword is what you want, it matters little of what kind or of what colour the sheath may be.

82. The methods of a Sādhū should be those of a winnowing fan; he should lay hold of the weighty matters and let subjects of little moment fly away.

83. Kabīr says; to associate with a Sādhū is like sitting near a seller of perfumes; though the seller sell you nought, yet you enjoy the scent of his perfumes.

84. As as ant is carrying off a grain of rice, it falls in with a grain of *dāl*. Kabīr says; both you cannot carry away, take the one and leave the other.

85. A madman was beating the hole of a snake, but the snake was not hit; fool, it is not the snake's hole that bites; it is the snake that devours men.

86. Where is the boundary of the heavens? What is the weight of the world? What is the caste of a Sādhū ? What is the price of the Alchemist's stone ?

87. The dog of a Sādhū is virtuous, while evil is the mother of

one who becomes not the chela of a guru; the one sits and hears the praises of Hari; the other speaks evil of gurus.

88. Learn to distinguish the honest man and the thief from their manner of speech, all the works that are within proceed forth by way of the mouth. Cf St Matt. xii 34. Out of the abundance of the heart the mouth speaketh.

89. In the midst of the highest heaven there is a shining light; he who has no guru cannot reach the palace; he only will reach it who is under the guidance of a true Guru.

90. Feel no care; be free from care; the giver is powerful; the beasts of the field, the birds and the insects have neither wealth nor store house.

91. The tortoise takes care of its egg; without breasts it supplies its needs; so God provides for all and makes provision for the three *lokas* (earth, heaven and hell).

92. Whatever I did, you did; I did nothing myself: should man say, I did it, it was in your strength that it was done. Cf. Phil. ii. 13.

Shāms Tabrez, the famous Sūfi, is said to have raised a man from the dead. Three times he addressed the corpse, saying. In the name of God, I bid three rise. These words had no effect. He then said. 'In my name I bid thee rise' and the man rose. The idea is that man's real power lies in the consciousness of his union with God. So long as he addressed God as one apart from himself, his prayer was disregarded.

93. Everything is from God and nothing from his servant; he can change a mustard seed into a mountain and a mountain into a mustard seed.

94. Should all the earth be turned into paper and all the trees into pens; should the seven seas be turned into ink, yet could not an account of God be written.

95. In blessings, O God, thou surpassest all, in thy dealings with men thou art without a rival; God is chief of all kings, and yet He lived upon earth as a *faqīr*.

96. We shall not die, though all creation die; we have found one that quickeneth.

These lines form part of an introduction to a *Bhajan*.

97. Whoever forsakes what is false and productive of pride and becomes as dust on the road, he will find God.

98. The difference between the true and the false Sādhū is as that between the Ām (mango) and the Babūl trees; the former bears

life-producing fruit, the latter thorns.

Phal (fruit) is often used of the results of action.

99. When you see a Sādhū approaching, run, touch with your hands his feet (and apply them to your forehead). It may be that in this form God himself will meet you.

100. All say 'Rām, Rām', but there is a difference in the saying; one associated with many, another was absorbed in one.

The writer seems to be here distinguishing between Rām, the son of Daśrāth, and Rām, as used as a title of the one true God.

101. O Nārāyan, there have been countless mighty rulers in this world; they used to speak of I and mine, but when they died they took not away with them a single straw.

102. If a man be meek, humble, respectful and obedient to Sādhūs, in his heart I dwell, as a fish dwells in the water.

103. What stays not at a high level, but descends; he who stoops down can raise up the water and drink; he who remains standing must go away with thirst unquenched.

104. Only the guru is found, but no disciple (every one presumes to teach, none are willing to learn); there is some hope of success, when a disciple is found.

105. What is the use of greatness? the palm is a tall tree, but none sit under its shade and its fruit is out of reach.

106. If you wish to worship Rām, worship him at once; when will you find another opportunity ? The grass that now is fresh and green will shortly be dried as fuel.

107. Thou camest into this world for gain; gamble not away thy life, weigh carefully in thy mind, this moment will not return again.

CHAPTER 5

The Kabīr Panth

THE Kabīr Panthis of northern and central India recognise two main divisions of the Panth, one with headquarters at the Kabīr Chaura in Benares and a branch establishment at Maghar, and a second, founded by Dharm Dāss, with headquarters in the Chattisgarh district, in the Central Provinces. The former is known as *bāp* (father) and the latter as *mai* (mother). The relations between these two divisions have at times been strained. The Maṭh at Puri, where, in the worship of Jagannāth, distinctions of caste are disregarded, is respected by both as a place of pilgrimage.[1]

It is impossible in the light of present information to determine the date at which either of these divisions first came into existence, but both were probably founded by Hindu disciples of Kabir.

As already stated Kabīr died and was buried at Maghar, in the district of Gorakhpur. The shrine at Maghar which has always been in the charge of Muhammadans was restored in 1567 by Nawab Fidae Khān, the officer in command of the imperial army which occupied the city in that year.[2]

There are at the present time two Maṭhs at Maghar, one for Muhammadans, containing the shrine, and another for Hindus, in the enclosure of which is a hole in which Kabīr is said to have sat, awaiting death.[3] Each of these Maṭhs which adjoin one another,

---

[1]The division of the Panth into twelve branches, as given in Wilson *Religious Sects of the Hindus* seems to be quite fanciful. There are other branches at Bombay, in Gujarat, etc. but it is doubtful whether these regard themselves as independent of these two main divisions. Of these two divisions, that which bears the name of Dharm Dāss, though barely mentioned by Wilson, is the more influential at the present time.

[2]From 1300 to 1567 AD. Maghar was the capital of the Samet Rajpūts.

[3]It is stated in the *Basti Gazetteer* that a Hindu Mahant first arrived at Maghar in 1764 AD. According to Kabīr Chaurā traditions the first four Mahants were buried at Maghar.

has accommodation for 50 Sādhūs, though as a rule only one Fakir
or Sadhū lives in each.[1] About 50 Hindū Sādhus live in the neighbouring villages of Balwā and Khurswal where the Panth has
property in land.[2]

At Maghar there are more Muhammadan than Hindu Kabīr
Panthis. The two sections have little in common, except their devotion to Kabīr their Master. Each section receives *Prasād* in its
own Maṭh.

In connexion with the Muhammadan Maṭh a largely attended
Melā is held on the last day of Aghan (November). In connexion
with this Melā a sacred feast is held. The Mahant proceeds to the
shrine, followed by the Dīwān, carrying in both hands a large dish
(*thambe*) containing *Khichri* (cooked rice mixed with *dāl*) and by
a *Bandālī* carrying an earthenware vessel (*karwā*) containing water
and covered over with a white cloth. Upon reaching the shrine
these vessels are placed upon the ground and frankincense is burnt
upon the tomb, in a fire of cowdung.[3] The Mahant repeats certain
prayers in which all present take their part.[4]

At the conclusion of the prayers he takes his seat upon the ground
while the Dīwān gives to each of the worshippers a small portion of
the *Khichri* and the Bandālī pours from the spout of the *Kaṛwā* a
few drops of the water into the palm of their hands. When all have
received, the Dīwān and Bandāli consume what is left. More prayers
are said, after which the Mahant departs and the gathering
breaks up.[5]

Pilgrims to the shrine are expected to present a rupee to the
officer in charge and also an offering of rice and *dāl*. They receive

---

[1] The Hindu Maṭh is under the management of the Kabīr Chaura Mahant.
The present Mahant, Gur Prasad Dass, is specially interested in the superinten-
dence of agricultural operations. In the absence of the Mahant the Pujāri is
placed in charge of the Kabīr Chaurā Maṭh.

[2] This land is chiefly under rice cultivation. In 1900 the land at Balwa supplied
the Kabir Chaura Maṭh with 750 maunds of rice and the Maghar Maṭh with
500 maunds.

[3] These ashes are passed through fine muslin and preserved in a brass *lotā*.

[4] The Kabīr Panthis apply the term prayer to devotional exercises which might
be more accurately described as meditations.

[5] It seemed best to describe this feast here and so complete the account relating to Maghar. The religious feasts of the Hindu Kabīr Panthis, which are
conducted with considerably more ritual, are described in Chapter 6.

in return a small portion of *Khichri* and a pinch of the ashes that result from the burning of the frankincense and cowdung.[1]

The Kabīr Chaura Maṭh receives its name from the fact that it occupies the site upon which according to tradition Kabīr gave instruction to his disciples. The Maṭh consists of two courtyards, connected by a bridge thrown across a narrow lane. The main courtyard contains the preaching platform, the *Mandar*, which is occupied by a pair of wooden sandals (*khaṇaū*) intended to represent the feet of the Guru,[2] the *Gaddi*,[3] the *Samādhis* (tombs)[4] of five Mahants and quarters for Sādhūs. The courtyard across the lane which occupies the traditional site of Nīru's house is made over to the female Bairāgis, known as *Mai Log*.[5] This court contains the Samadhīs of three Mahants.

The room in which the Gaddi is placed in immediately opposite the entrance gate. Over the Gaddī hangs the picture of Kabīr which has been reproduced as the frontispiece of this volume. In this picture Sūrat Gopāl and Dharm Dāss, the founders of the two main divisions of the Panth, are represented as kneeling before Kabīr while Kamāl stands behind with a fan in his hand. On one side of the picture hangs a portrait of Rāmānand and on the other

[1]The Muhammadan members of the Panth wear caps of a different shape to those worn by the Hindu bairāgis.

[2]Originally there was no Mandar (temple) at Kabir Chaura, but in this respect, as probably in others, the Kabīr Panthis have gradually assimilated their own arrangements to those of the Maṭhs of other religious orders. The *Dasnāmis* worship the feet of Śankarāchārya, carved in ontline in stone or marble. It was probably in order to escape the charge of idolatry that the Kabīr Panthis substituted for the *Charan Pādukā* a pair of wooden sandals.

[3]The *Gaddī* is literally the pillow upon which the Guru sits in state. The *Gaddi* of this Maṭh belongs to Kabīr, his representative upon earth sits behind and not upon it.

[4]When practicable the Mahants are buried within the precincts of their Maṭh. It is the custom of this, as of several other religious orders to bury and not burn the bodies of their dead. The custom which may be due to Muhammadan influences is explained by saying that the bodies of Sants who have died to the world have already been purified and do not require the cleansing of fire.

[5]The female devotees are given the title of mother because all Sādhus are required to treat them with the respect due to a mother from her son. When a married man is received into the order of the *Dandās* he applies his lips to the breast of his wife to indicate that heneeforth he stands to her in the relation of son to mother.

a picture of Rangi Dāss, the late Mahant, who died eight years ago.

Above the pictures are hung what appear from the distance to be armorial bearings, but are in reality designs in coloured cloth, intended to symbolise the five elements (earth, air, fire, water and *akāśa* and the nine doors or points of entrance into the human body. In front of the Gaddī are placed two flower-vases and upon the wall at the side hangs a rosary, composed of a thousand beads, which is reserved for the use of Mahant.

Daily service is conducted in the Math, morning and evening, by the *pujārī*. In the morning the Sādhūs, so soon as they have bathed, assemble in front of the Mandar. Here takes place the first part of the service which includes the performance of *Ārtī*[1] and the washing of the Guru's feet. After this the various Samādhis and the Gaddi are visited and the Sādhūs return to the Mandar for the concluding portion of the service. The morning service is said to occupy thirty minutes and the evening service an hour.

The water in which the wooden sandals have been washed, known as *Charan Amrita*, is poured into a brazen vessel. Three teaspoonfuls of this water together with three *tulsi*[2] leaves, are given to all who visit the Math during the day. At 8 p.m. the doors of the Math are closed and any *Charan Amrita* that remains over is offered in the first place to such Sādhus as have not previously received it. The vessel is then presented to the Mahant who after drinking what remains rinses out the vessel with fresh water and consumes that also.

An annual Melā which lasts over four or five days is held at this Math in the month of January. On this occasion the large courtyard is crowded with devotees. Those who wish to become Bairāgis observe a fast for twelve days, eating in the evening a little *gur* (crude sugar) and rice cooked in milk. These candidates are admitted as Bairāgis at the celebration of the *Jot Pershād*, which, from a religious point of view, constitutes the principal purpose of

---

[1] In Arti fire, usually the flames of burning camphor, is waved before the object of worship.

[2] The Tulsī leaf is sacred to Vishṇu. Many Kabīr Panthis feel that in thus showing reference to Vishṇu they are disregarding the teaching of Kabīr, as by Rām he meant not the incarnation of Vishṇu but the supreme Deity.

A group of Kabir Panthis, in camp at the Magh Mela, Allahabad.

(to face p. 61)

the Melā.[1]. Of the possessions belonging to the Maṭh the Kabīr Panthis regard the ṭopī (cap) and sehlī woollen necklace of Kabīr, the Kaṇau, the picture of Kabīr and the Bījak as those of greatest value.

The principal officers of the Maṭh are the Mahant, the Dīwān, the Kotwāl and the Pujāri. The Mahant is responsible for the general arrangements and should be a man of learning, qualified to give religious instruction; the Diwān is the business manager; the Kotwāl is responsible for the maintenance of discipline, while the Pujārī conducts the pūjā (worship) and keeps clean and in order the Mandar and the Gaddi.

The headquarters of the Dharm Dāss section were originally at Bāndogarh in the neighbourhood of Jubulpure; from this place they were transferred to Koodarmāl and once again in recent years to Dhāma Kherā.

Dharm Dāss, the founder of this section, is said to have first met Kabīr at Benares and to have been rebuked by him for worshipping idols. He met him subsequently at Brindāban, but failing to recognise him said, "Your words resemble those addressed to me by a Sādhū whom I once met at Benares." On this occasion Kabīr adopted stronger measures and threw into the river the idol which Dharm Dāss was worshipping. Once more Kabīr appeared to him in his house at Bāndogarh. Dharm Dāss was a bunniāh by caste and possessed of considerable wealth. Kabīr again rebuked him for practising idolatry and asked him how he could worship an idol made out of the same stone as the weights which he made use of in his business. On this occasion Dharm Dāss acknowledged the force of his arguments and both he and his wife became his disciples. According to the account given in Sūkrit Dhyān Dharm Dāss was the son of one Mahesh, and was as an infant saved from death by Gyāni (i.e. Kabīr) who entered into his body. He was originally called Judāwan, but objected to this name and received from Kabīr permission to change it to Dharm Dāss. Nārāyan

---

[1]It is said that the Jot Pershād was originally celebrated in this Maṭh once a month, but that this custom was discontinued on account of a quarrel that arose between Pūran Dāss and the contemporary Mahant of the Dharm Dāss section, in consequence of which the latter refused to supply Pūran Dāss with something which was regarded as essential for the proper conduct of this service. For an account of the Jot Pershād see Chapter 6.

Dāss, his son, refused to accept Kabīr as his Guru, but through the grace of Kabīr a second son was born in 1516 and named Churāman.[1] This son was installed upon the Gaddī by Kabīr himself. Upon the occasion of his installation Kabīr foretold that his descendants should sit upon the Gaddī for 42 generations (*Bans*), and declared that the right to communicate the *Mantra* would be confined to his descendants. In accordance with Kabīr's instructions the Head Mahant of this section marries and lives with his wife till a son is born. After the birth of the son the wife becomes a *Bairāgi*. The Mahant holds office for a period of 25 years and 20 days and is then succeeded by his son.[2] In one case the son is said to have died and as the mother had become a *Bairāgi* the Mahant lived with another woman by whom he had a son.[3] The father of the present Mahant died after holding office for a period of three years only, and many wished that one of his disciples, Jugla Nand, should officiate as Mahant during the remainder of his term of office. To this proposal the majority of the members strongly objected on the ground that he was not a descendant of Dharm Dāss, and Ugranām was duly installed. His grandmother, known as Dādi Sāhib, who was responsible for this proposal, still exercises authority at Koodarmal, and Ugranām reigns in the newly established Maṭh at Dhāma Kherā. Jugla Nand with other discontented Sādhūs retired to Bombay, where he has published various books bearing upon the Panth. Kabīr is said to have given instructions to Dharm Dāss regarding the *Chaukā* and the *Jot Prasād*.

The Kabīr Panth exists as a protest against the religious exclusiveness of the twice-born castes. As a natural result few but Sūdras

---

[1] This date has apparently been chosen to bring the birth of Churāmān within the lifetime of Kabir. No mention is made of the age at which Churaman was installed as Mahant, No importance can be attached to dates mentioned in connexion with the establishment of the Panth. Ugranām is said to be the 13th Mahant. If eleven Mahants occupied the Gaddi for twenty years each and one Mahant for three the Panth would appear to have been founded 278 years previous to the installation of Ugranām, *i.e.* about 1625.

[2] The Mahant's son alone is a member of the Panth by birth and is initiated by his father. All other members become the children of the Mahant through the reception of the *Mantra*.

[3] The boy who died is said to have been Churaman who returned to the world, but retired after a short stay as he was unwilling a second time to sit upon the *gaddi*.

whose cause it champions have associated themselves with the movement. The Panth contends for a truth which forms part of the Gospel of Creation, viz. that all men have spiritual powers which should find their natural expression in communion with God, now in this life.[1]

The sons of the twice-born as they come to years of discretion are invested with the sacred thread (*janeo*) and reminded thereby of their spiritual privileges and responsibilities. The members of this Panth wear round their necks a *kaṇṭhi* (rosary) formed of beads made of Tulsi wood.[2] This *kaṇṭhi* is naturally associated with thoughts of prayer and in this way reminds those who wear it alike of their relation to God and of the promises which they made at the time of their initiation.[3] Permission to wear a *kaṇṭhi* is granted to women as well as to men, for they too are spiritual beings; but no woman may assume a *kaṇṭhi* previous to marriage nor may she become the disciple of her husband's Guru.[4]

---

[1] The exclusive spirit which finds expression in caste and against which Kabīr and other fought, has by no means been expelled from the minds of *Kabīr Panthis*. Members of the lowest castes, such as mehtars, doms and dhobis, should, they consider, join fects such as that of *Shiva Narayan* and not be permitted to wear *kanthis*.

[2] The *kaṇṭhi* of the *Kabīr Panthis* is formed of beads made of Tulsi wood, which are usually strung on string of very inferior quantity. This defect may result in the loss of the beads, and no member of the Panth is under such circumstance allowed to worship or eat food till the beads have been replaced. They are however, allowed to wear instead of the *kaṇṭhi* one large bead (*hira*) strong on substantial thread. Those who live in places where a lost *kaṇṭhi* cannot be easily replaced usually avail themselves of this alternative. Some *kaṇṭhis* are made of material other than wood. eg. grass or cocoanut fibre. Some *Satnamis* wear a wristlet made of string in lieu of a *kaṇṭhi*.

[3] Prayer as offered by the *Kabīr Panthis* is of an elementary character. One says that they pray that they may obtain salvation (*mukti*); another says that he sings the praises of Narayan in the morning and in the evening prays for protection against evil spirits. The latter spoke of our Church Services as 'practice', and regarded them as valuable in as much as they helped to form a habit of punctuality. It would be a great mistake to suppose that prayer means for a *Kabīr Panthi* the same as it does for a Christian.

At the time of prayer members of the Panth make on their forehead the mark (*Tilak*) of Vishṇu, using for the purpose a special kind of earth mixed with water or with water only.

[4] If disciples of the same Guru they would be regarded as brother and sister and so their marriage would become unlawful. This, however, appears to be a

To Brahmins at the time of investiture with the sacred thread is communicated the Brahminical *mantra* which they are not allowed on any account to communicate to those who are not Brahmins.[1] In like manner at the time of initiation a *mantra* is whispered into the ear of Kabīr Panthis. This Mantra serves as a bond of union between members of the Panth and also suggests a position of privilege.[2]

Brahmins wear upon their forehead the sign of the God whom they worship. Kabīr Panthis also wear such a mark (*tīkā*), as shown in the frontispiece.

In the days of Kabīr a knowledge of religious truth was practically confined to those who were acquainted with one or other of the two sacred languages, Arabic and Sanskrit. These two languages were employed both in public and private worship with the result that the worship of the masses was too often a mere repetition of phrases which were unintelligible to those who used them. Kabīr urged that religious books should also be written in the vernacular that all might obtain that knowledge of God which was essential to spiritual progress.

Again to the illiterate masses teaching contained in books was inaccessible, and so it is that we find Kabīr laying great stress on the importance of oral teaching. Few men are qualified to become scholars, but all are required to be good: therefore he urged his disciples to associate with good men and through conversation with them to acquire such knowledge as is necessary. The study of books, he thought, was too often productive of pride; to display learning

---

later refinement as Dharm Dass and his wife were both the disciples of Kabīr. They would probably argue that this was a matter of necessity, as at that time there was only one Guru whereas in modern days there are many.

[1] The spiritual life of Brāhmins, Kshattriyas and Vaishyas is recognised from the time when they receive the *mantra* from their Guru and are invested with the sacred thread. From that time they are subject to the rules of caste, only those who have reached years of discretion are admitted as members of the *Panth* with the possible exception of children, both of whose parents are already members.

[2] The initiatory Mantra of the Kabīr Panth is said to contain five words which represent one name or revelation of the one true God. Should the *chelā* at the time of initiation fail to catch the words on account of nervousness or the noise of music, he may have it repeated to him by some other member of the Panth, provided that this is done in a solitary place where there is no chance of the words being overheard by others.

and intelligence scholars were often tempted to enlarge upon topics of little spiritual value, while in private conversation heart speaks to heart of its own spiritual needs. Such were the views of Kabīr and in consequence the Guru in this Panth occupies a position of extraordinary importance.

Kabīr was a poet of no mean order and gladly consecrated his literary gifts to the service of God. He knew that religious instruction given in the form of poetry was easily remembered; he knew too that the singing of *bhajans* (hymns) was an occupation in which the people of India took peculiar pleasure. It only remained for him to compose hymns which his followers could sing. This he did, and up to the present day his hymns enjoy great popularity with the people and in the Panth occupy a prominent position in all acts of public worship.

As the Brāhmins are required to repeat the Gyatri daily, so are members of this Panth required to use the following hymns, in the morning and evening respectively :

Morning Hymn—Kabīr said, Spiritual and material blessings attend those who wait upon the Darwesh; their account is safe. Love of you pervades the whole body of your devotees. You are starvation, unmoved by desire, a mendicant. You walk in no one's footsteps, you seek case in no abode. The whole universe is your body. You are boundless (a stream without banks). You pervade the Universe constantly. The love which you cause is profound. The empty Universe is in me, says the Guru (Kabīr). If we do honour by fire to the true name, the body becomes pure. Dharam Dāss taking the Guru's arm walked and found Kabīr.

Evening Hymn—Evening having come on, the day having closed, the duck broke into wailing : "O drake, let us go to that country where day and night are unknown." If separation takes place at night, the duck is to be met with in the morning, but he who is separated from the name (of God) regains it neither during day nor night. Hear, O Guru, Treasury of kindness, I beseech you with clasped hands. Mercy, humility, devotion, equality, good nature, constancy, these are the ornaments of a devotee. Devotion to the one without beginning is adornment. The only name, the only Guru, is Kabīr, the highest *Pīr*.[1]

[1] For these *bhajans* in their original form see Crooke's *Tribes and Castes of N.W.P. and Oudh*, vol. III, pp 75 76. For the translation in the text I am indebted to a resident of Kanpur who locally enjoys a reputation as a Hindi poet.

Anxious as Kabīr was to claim for all men spiritual privleges he was no less anxious to impress upon those who desired to become religious that they must live in a way consistent with their profession.

All, therefore, who desire to become members of the *Panth* are required to renounce polytheism and to acknowledge their belief in one only God (*Parameshwar*). They must also promise to eat no meat and drink no wine; to bathe daily and sing hymns to God, both morning and evening; to forgive those who trespass against them up to three times; to avoid the company of all women of bad character and all unseemly jesting in connexion with such subjects; never to turn away from their house their lawful wife; never to tell lies; never to conceal the property of another man; never to bear false witness against a neighbour or speak evil of another on hearsay evidence.[1]

One prominent trait in Hindu character, viz. personal devotion, finds ample scope for exercise in the devotion to their Guru required of all members of the Panth. All who wish to approach God must, they say, become the disciple of some Guru and to this Guru when once chosen, the disciple must wholly submit himself, mind, soul and body. To Kabīr, as the chief Guru, many of the *bhajans* used in public worship are addressed, and marked reverence is also shown to the living Guru, as God's representative upon earth.

---

[1]In requiring such promises from his followers Kabīr doubtless indicates those defects in Hindu social life which to him appeared most detrimental to the development of religion. To the promise to eat no meat the greatest importance is attached in all the Vaishnavite sects as such a habit is supposed to develop the material and injure the spiritual part of human nature. This belief with reference to eating flesh makes them slow to realise that Christianity, which regards such questions as matters of indifference can really a spiritual force.

List of the Kabīr Chaurā Mahants

Name of Mahant	Samādhi at	Years of office	Approximate date of Installation
Shyām Dāss	Maghar	28	1491 ?
Lāl Dāss	Maghar	22	1519 ?
Hari Dāss	Maghar	18	1541 ?
Surat Gopāl Dāss	Jagannāth	35	1559
Gyān Dāss	Jagannāth	25	1594
Sital Dāss	Gayā	24	1619
Sukh Dāss	Nirū Tila	20	1643
Hulāss Dāss	Nirū Tila	26	1663
Mādho Dāss	Nirū Tila	20	1689
Kokil Dāss	Nirū Tila	21	1709
Rām Dāss	Nirū Tila	29	1730
Mahā Dāss	Nirū Tila	22	1759
Hari Dāss	Nirū Tila	20	1781
Sukh Dāss	Kabīr Chaurā	27	1801
Saran Dāss	Kabīr Chaurā	16	1828
Puran Dāss	Kabīr Chaurā	18	1844
Nirmal Dāss	Kabīr Chaurā	22	1862
Ranghir Dāss	Kabīr Chaurā	15	1884
Gur Prasād Dāss		8	1899

The above list so far as the name of Mahant, place of Samādh and tenure of office are concerned was supplied by a Bairāgi at Benares.

The existence of the first three Mahants is highly problematical.

Surat Gopāl (AD 1559) is generally regarded as the founder of the Panth. It is possible that he and the two Mahants who succeeded him did not have their headquarters at Benares, but that the Nirū Ṭīlā compound was acquired during the Mahanti of Sukh Dāss. Bulwant Singh, and his son and successor, Cheit Singh, were patrons of the Kabīr Panth. The former died in AD 1770. The Kabīr Chaurā Compound may have been acquired in their time.

Though seven Mahants are said to, have been buried in the Nirū

Tīlā court of the Maṭh at Benares only three Samādhis are conspicuous at the present time. (see p. 59)

List of Dharam Dāss Mahants

Name		Approximate date of Installation
Chūrāmaṇi	Nām	1694
Sūdarshan	Nām	1714
Kulpati	Nām	1734
Pramodh	Nām Gurū Bālā Pīr	1754
Kewal	Nām	1774
Amol	Nām	1794
Surat Sanehi	Nām	1814
Haqq	Nām	1834
Pāk	Nām	1854
Praghat	Nām	1874
Dhīraj	Nām	1894
Ugrā	Nām	1897
Dayā	Nām	

The above have already appeared. Those follow are :

Gridhmanī Nām	Akah Nām
Prakāsh Nām	Kanthmani Nām
Uditmanī Nām	Santokh Nām
Mukundmanī Nām	Chātrik Nām
Adh Nām	Dadhi Nām
Udai Nām	Neh Nām
Gyān Nām	Adī Nām
Hansmani Nām	Mahā Nām
Sukrit Nām	Nij Nām
Agrmanī Nām	Sāhib Dāss Nām
Ras Nām	Udhawa Dāss Nām
Gungmani Nām	Karunra Nām
Pāras Nām	Uddhar Nām
Jāgrat Nām	Drigh Nām
Bhringhmani Nām	Mahāmanī Nām

The dates have been calculated on the assumption that each Mahant held office for 20 years and 25 days, except Dhīraj Nām who is known to have died after three years tenure of office. One Mahant stated that the regular tenure of office was for 25 years and 20 days. On such a calculation the date of Churāmanī would be thrown back to AD 1654. In the Kabīr Chaurā section the average tenure of office has been for 23 years.

The *Sukh Nidhān* is said to have been written during Pramodh Nām's tenure of office.

CHAPTER 6

The Kabīr Panth (*Contd.*)

THIS Panth, like other religious institutions of the kind, is founded on a double basis. Members may live as householders in
their own homes, or renounce the world and attach themselves
permanently to one of the Monasteries belonging to the order.
Those belonging to the latter class are known as Bairāgis. A married man may leave his wife, whom he is henceforth to regard as
his mother, and become a Bairāgi, provided that he is the father of
at least one son. Women, as well as men, may become Bairāgis, if
found properly qualified after a probationary period of two years.[1]
Conventual buildings exist both at Kabīr Chaurā and Maghar. The
householders perform an important function in the economy of
the order, inasmuch as they contribute largely to the support of
the Bairāgis.

There are a large number of branch establishments, each of
which is presided over by a Mahant who spends most of his time
in travelling round to visit the disciples who acknowledge him as
their *Guru*.[2] He is supposed to visit his *Chelās* at least once a year,
to note the progress they have made, to give instruction to them
and to their families, and to exomine and to receive into the order,
if found qualified, such candidates as may be brought to him. On
such occasions he is entertained by members of the Panth and also
provided with travelling expenses.

The Mahants of the branch establishments receive authority to
teach and initiate new members from the Head Mahant of the
section to which they belong. At the time of appointment they are
given to eat a betel leaf (*bīṛā*)[3] as a pledge that they undertake

[1]Female Bairagis are usually widows or the wives of men who have become
Bairagis. At Maghar there are said to be about 25 female Bairāgis.

[2]The Mahants are not allowed to shave; the Bairāgis must either shave entirely or not at all.

[3]In ancient days a *pan* leaf (*Bīṛā*) was thrown down as a challenge. This
custom is referred to in the *Rāmāyaṇa*.

faithfully to perform the duties of their office.[1] Each Mahant receives a document, bearing the seal of the Head Mahant, and known as the *Panja Parwāna.* Upon this document are entered the names of all disciples admitted by him into the order. The Mahant is required to check this list at each place that he visits and to present it annually to the Head Mahant both for inspection and the entry of new names.[2]

As signs of authority the Mahant receives a red *topi*, a necklace of black wool, known as *Seli*,[3] and a special rosary known as the *Pānch Māl.*

On the occasion of his annual visit to Headquarters the Mahant is required to present twelve cocoanuts and twelve rupees on his own account and one cocoanut and one rupee for each new name that he wishes to have entered on his Parwāna. He also makes over to the Diwān all offerings made at the Chaukā Ārti services at which he has officiated during the year.

A Mahant upon appointment is required to make an offering of cocoanuts. Kabīr Panthis explain the peculiar significance attached to cocoanuts in the Panth in the light of the following facts: (1) it has a face resembling that of a man, (2) its surface is divided into three parts recalling Brahmā, Śiva and Viṣṇu, (3) its flesh is formed gradually as human flesh is formed and (4) it differs from other fruits in containing no seed.[4] The breaking of the cocoanut is regarded as a bloodless sacrifice, a peace offering presented to Niranjan to secure for members of the Panth admission into heaven.

---

[1]One of the Mahants at Lucknow assumed office when 14 years of age. Normally when a minor is nominated for succession an unbeneficed Mahant is associated with him in office, till he is able to perform the duties unassisted.

[2]On the occasion of a visit to any place the Mahant recites at celebration of the *Chaukā Ārti* all the names entered either upon his own *Parwāna* or those of his predecessors in office, and writes the words *Chalana kar gayā* against the names of any who have died. In the case of a deceased Mahant the phrase used is *Samādhi le li.*

[3]The *Seli* is very similar to that worn by certain followers of Nānak. In each case there are five tassels attached to the *Seli.* In the Kabīr Panth *Seli* there are three tassels placed together in the centre with one on either side; in the Nānak *Seli* the five tassels are placed at regular intervals. For shape of *Topi* see frontispiece.

[4]Do they wish to imply that the cocoanut represents God made man, the word become flesh?

The ordinary Mahants are not men of great learning, though they have usually committed to memory a certain number of sayings attributed to Kabīr and possibly also some book of which they have managed to secure a copy. Want of learning is in some sort atoned for in the opinion of their followers by a detailed knowledge of the ritual to be observed in the performance of religious ceremonies. The more learned Mahants have generally some knowledge of Tulsī Dāss's *Rāmāyaṇa* and *The Bhagawad Gītā*.

Before giving an account of the ceremony of initiation and the two sacramental meals, the *Chaukā Ārtī* and the *Jot Prasād*, it seems best to explain two terms which are especially associated with the initiation ceremony and the *Jot Prasād*. The two terms in question are *Charan Amrita* and *Parwāna*.

Charan Amriṭa, the *amrita* of the feet, is the name given to the water in which have been washed the feet of the Head Mahant, Kabīr's representative upon earth. This water is mixed with fine earth and then made up into pills. These pills may either be swallowed whole, or pounded up, mixed with water and drunk.

Parwāna (passport) is the name given to the betel leaf specially prepared at head quarters at the time of a celebration of the *Jot Prasād*. A pile of betel leaves, sixteen handbreadths in height is arranged upon the ground. At night time a pewter saucer is placed upon a specially prepared spot and the dew collected in this vessel is known as *amar*, water derived from heaven direct. In the morning the Mahant meditates in front of the pile of betel leaves and with the *amar* writes upon the topmost leaves the secret name of God. The betel leaves thus consecrated are made up into small portions, about a quarter of an inch square, and distributed among the Mahants for use at a celebration of the *Jot Prasād* or for presentation to a candidate at the time of his initiation. The *Parwānā* is said to represent the body of Kabīr.

The ceremony of initiation is one of considerable solemnity. The candidate in the presence of the Guru and other members of the *Panth* makes the required promises and is solemnly warned as to the consequences for good or evil that will depend upon the way in which he afterwards observes them.[1] While *bhajans* are being

---

[1] Most members fear to violate promises made in so solemn a manner, lest the wrath of God should fall upon them. It is said that one, a seller of oil, drank some wine and eat some flesh. He was expelled from the Panth and immediately fell ill. After six months he recovered and was readmitted into the

sung by those present half of the mantra is whispered into the left
ear of the candidate by the Gurū, who afterwards places in his two
outstretched hands, placed together, some grass, *pān* leaves and
white flowers. A Bairāgi, taking a brass vessel containing water in
one hand, with the other leads the candidate to another quarter of
the room where he allows the grass, etc. to fall upon the ground.
Having moved a short way from that spot the candidate again
places his hands together and into them the Bairāgi pours water
from the vessel. With the first handful of water he rinses out his
mouth; with the second he washes his face. After this the candidate
is led back to the Guru. The Gurū takes up a *kanthi* and makes it
over to a Bairāgi who takes it round the assembly and presents it
to all members of the Panth in turn. All touch it with their hands
and it is then returned by the Bairāgi to the Mahant.[1] The Mahant
placing the *kanthi* in his open hands does obeisance to the Gaddi
and then stretching it between the thumb and first finger of both
hands lets it fall over the head on to the neck of the candidate, as
he kneels before him.[2] At the conclusion of this ceremony he whis-
pers the whole *mantra* into the right ear of the candidate.[3] So soon
as the *mantra* has been communicated the new disciple is warned
that he must on no account eat the fruit of the fig tree (*gūlar*).
In reply to inquiries as to the reason for this prohibition, he is told
that the fruit contains many flies and cannot therefore be eaten
without much destruction of life. From amongst the articles of food

Panth, but after an interval of a year he repeated his offence and died in consequence. Another member who committed a similar offence is said to have
lost the use of a hand.

[1]This process is known as *Gawāhī* (witness).

[2]None but a Mahant may invest anyone with the kanthi of the order. A
Cawnpore Mahant once fell into the hands of the police who at once destroyed
his kanthi. As soon as the Mahant recovered his freedom he invested himself
with a second kanthi. This irregularity was at once reported to the Head
Mahant and the offender and another member of the Panth who was supposed
to have connived at his offence, were immediately excommunicated.

[3]In the Kabīr Chaura section only one mantra is communicated to the
candidate, viz. the Guru Mantra. In the Dharam Dāss section two mantras are
communicated at the time of initiation, the Guru Mantra and the Tinkā Arpan
mantra, and three more subsequently in response to inquiry, viz. the Pānch
Nām Sat Nām and the Har Nām. The Gurū Mantra in use in the two sections
is said to be different in form. In the Kabīr Chaurā section any reference to
Dharam Dāss is avoided as far as possible.

that have been placed beneath a clean cloth the Guru then takes
a cocoanut and places it in the two hands of the candidate who
touches with the fruit his right shoulder, his breast and forehead
and returns it to the Guru with a fee of one rupee. The Guru,
having washed the cocoanut with betel leaves dipped in water,
breaks it upon a stone. He proceeds with a knife to cut up the flesh
of the cocoanut into small portions and deposits them in an open
dish. He next pours into the hands of the candidate some *Charan
Amrit* which he reverently drinks. The Mahant then takes a *pān*
leaf and placing upon it a *parwāna*, a portion of cocoanut, some
batāsā, gūr,[1] raisins and currants, deposits it in the outstretched
hands of the candidate who transfers it to his mouth. After the
candidate has in this way been received into the Panth all members
present receive at the hands of the Guru a betel leaf upon, which is
placed a portion of the cocoanut, some *batāsā, gūr*, raisins and
currants. No portion of the cocoanut may be destroyed or eaten
by those who are not members of the *Panth*,[2] Any portion that
remains over is carefully preserved by the Guru and given to *Panthis* in other places that he may visit, with a statement as to the
name and residence of the new disciple at whose initiation it was
offered. This ceremony is followed by a feast, in which members
of other religious sects are also permitted to take part. Reverence
is paid to the Guru and Parameshwar and many *bhajans* are sung
in honour of Parameshwar and Kabīr.

This ceremony which in a measure corresponds to Christian
Baptism is known as *Tinka Arpan*. In the Dharam Dāss section the
candidate presents one cocoanut only and one money offering
which must not be less than one rupee. In the Kabīr Chaurā section
candidates are required to present no less than sixteen cocoanuts,
since they say sixteen sons (*sūt*) were begotten of the Word, and
with each cocoanut an offering of money which must not be less

---

[1]Batāsā is a small sugary wafer in common use at religious gatherings; *Gur*
is a preparation of sugar.

[2]A corresponding ceremony exists among other sects but different fruits are
used, e.g. the followers of Tulsī Dāss partake of a plaintain. One plantain only
only is used for this purpose. If many members are present, it is mixed with
other food till the quantity is sufficient. The *Rāmānandis* eat the leaf of the
Tulsī plant.

than four annas.[1] There is another important difference in the
practice of the two sections. In the Dharam Dāss section this ceremony *Tinkā Arpan*, may never be repeated, whereas in the Kabīr
Chaura section it is performed twice, once by the candidate's
personal Guru and again by the Head Mahant in the Kabīr Chaurā
Maṭh. This difference may in part be accounted for by the fact
that the Mahants of the Kabīr Chaurā section are not supplied with
a *parwāna* and also by the fact that in this section any Bairāgī is
authorised to initiate new members.

Every member of the *Panth* is required to supply the material
wants of his Guru to the best of his ability, and also to pray on
his behalf. As on account of such material help the Gurū is benefi-
ted by an increase in the member of his chelas, he is not himself
allowed to invite others to become members of the *Panth*.

As regards discipline, any disciple who brings discredit on the
Panth by irregularity of life or who in other ways offends against
the traditions of the order is in the first place censured by his Guru
and subsequently, should he refuse to listen to advice, excluded
from all religious gatherings. His company is avoided by other
members of the Panth and his salutations disregarded by the Guru.

The ordinary members of the *Panth* believe that the souls of
Panthis after death enter Heaven (*baikunṭh*) or Hell (*narak*) and
there remain till they have been sufficiently rewarded or punished
for deeds done in the body. They then return to earth, but always
apparently clothed in a human body. This succession of lives continues till the soul freed from desire becomes absorbed in God. A
member of the *Panth* quoted to me the following saying attributed
to Nānak, "We want neither *baikunṭh* nor *narak*, but true life
(*pūrī zindagī*), and that is obtained when there are no more links
with this earth."[2]

Members of the *Kabīr Panth* are encouraged to observe every
Sunday as well as the last day of the lunar month (*Pūran Māsi*) as
a day of fasting, and having bathed to assemble at 8 o'clock in the
evening to join in a service, known as *chaukā*,[3] which takes the

---

[1] Of the sixteen cocoanuts four are broken at the *Tinka Arpan* ceremony, six
are sent to Maghar, and three are broken at each of the two Chaukā Ārtī ceremonies in the months of Phāgun and Bhādon.

[2] We may possibly in this belief see traces of Mohammadan or Christian
teaching.

[3] *Chaukā* is the term applied to the portion of ground specially prepared for

form of a religious meal.[1] A piece of ground measuring either 5
or 7 yards square is specially prepared and cleaned. In the centre
of this square is measured out a smaller space, 2½ yards square.
This inner square is covered over with flour, and in its centre are
placed some flowers[2] immediately in front of the service book
(*Puno Granth*). The Mahant sits in the enclosure. facing the con-
gregation, with the service book before him. On his right hand
within the smaller square are placed (i) a small metal box containing *Charan Amrita* and *Parwāna,* (ii) a dish containing 125 betel
leaves[3] arranged around the edge with a single leaf in the centre
on which is placed a piece of camphor, and (iii) a pillar composed
of dough, constructed with a hollow top, in the centre of which is
placed a stick enveloped in cotton wool. During the service *ghī*
is poured over this stick which is then lighted and serves as a

the consumption of food. The ground is divided up into squares, each one of
which is occupied by one person.

[1]All who attend the *chaukā* observe a fast throughout the preceding day, but
are allowed to drink water or water sweetened with sugar, if they find their thirst
oppressive. The majority of those who belong to the Panth are content to perform their devotions at home on Sundays and in this case only keep the fast up
to midday. The full *chaukā* service, followed by a meal as described below is
only performed of necessity on two occasions in the year, in the months of
Phāgun and *Bhādon,* which roughly correspond to March and August. On these
occasions the Mahant himself is necessarily present and all members are required to attend. Observanee of the whole day fast is a necessary condition of attendance at a Chaukā whether the Mahant is present or not.

[2]This specially prepared ground is covered over with an awning (*Chandwā*).
The colour of the awning, as well as that of the flowers, is white on festal occasions; red when the service, is held in memory of the dead. In addition to the
flowers that lie upon the *chaukā* a bunch of flowers is suspended from the centre
of the awning.

The *chaukā* is arranged by the Mahant. When he is not present the central
portion is not overlaid with flour; there is no box containing *Charan Amrita* and
Parwāna; in the place of the dough-made candle-stick is placed a dish on which
camphor is burnt, the water is placed in an ordinary *lotā* and not in a *kalsa,* for
the whole cocoanut are substituted fragments of cocoanut bought in the bazar.

The flour in the centre of the inner portion of the *chaukā* is fashioned to
represnt nine lotus flowers arranged in a circle. Upon these, which represent the
sun. moon and seven planets rest the natural flowers.

[3]To eat a betel leaf on such occasions is equivalent to taking a vow to loyally
observe the rules laid down. The Mahant removes to his own lodgings any betel
leaves that may be over from the *chaukā* service, but may only eat them himself
or give them to another member of the Panth.

candle throughout the ceremony. On the left hand of the Mahant
are placed (i) a dish containing *batāsā* and *gūr*, (ii) a cocoanut and
(iii) a brazen vessel (*kalaśa*) containing water.

At each corner of the inner portion of the *chaukā* is placed a
small earthenware jar containing water; on this jar rests an earthenware plate containing grain, and over this is placed a lamp (*chirāgh*)
fed with linseed oil.[1]

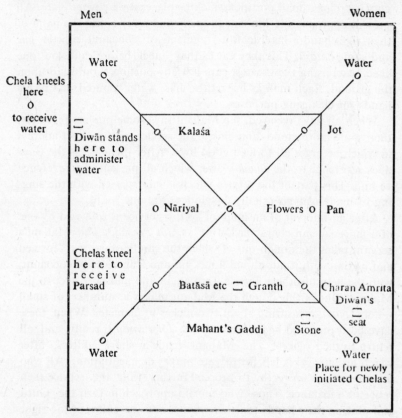

The Mahant, at the conclusion of the service, which he reads out
of the book, lights the candle which stands in the centre of the can-
dlestick made of dough. He next lights a piece of camphor on a

[1]The grain in the plate is to absorb any oil that may fall from the lamp and
so preserve the purity of the water. There is a similar arrangement in the case
of the *kalaśa*. The water in the earthenware vessels is used should the supply
of water in the *kalaśa* (a large round brazen vessel) prove insufficient.

stone that is set beside him and taking the cocoanut pours water
over it and then breaks it upon the stone,[1] and finally lights the
piece of camphor in the centre of the *pān* dish and while the camphor is burning waves it backwards and forwards (*ārtī*). The dish
is then passed round and those present place in it a small offering.
These offerings are taken by the Mahant for the use of his Maṭh.
He then takes half of the flesh of the cocoanut and with a penknife
cuts it up into small portions which he places on a pewter plate. All
present approach the Mahant in turn[2] and receive into the palm of
their right hand a betel leaf, a fragment of cocoanut, a little *gur*
and some *batāsā*. This they eat as they kneel before him on one
knee, exercising the greatest care lest any portion should fall upon
the ground. Each man as he retires has water poured upon his
hands for cleansing purposes.

When all have received, the Mahant says some prayers privately,
then some more aloud, and closes the service with a short address
in which he urges all to lead good lives. After the address the *Guru*
does reverence to the *chaukā*, after which all present do reverence
to him. This part of the service which is interspersed with the singing of many *bhajans* usually concludes at about 3 a.m.

After an interval of an hour or so this service is followed by one
of a more solemn character known as *Jot Prasād*.[3] The Mahant's
servant takes the dough out of which the candle-stand was formed
and mixing with it additional flour, *ghī* and fragments of cocoanut,
with the help of others kneeds it up again and makes it over to the
Mahant. Out of this dough the Mahant makes a number of small
wafers (*puri*), measuring about two inches in diameter. When these
have been prepared he calls aloud that *Jot Prasād* is ready, and all
return to their places. The Mahant reads a short address, after
which an interval is left for private prayer or meditation. All who
feel themselves unworthy to proceed further with the service then
retire to a distance. Those who remain approach in turn the Guru
and placing their hands together receive into the palm of the right

---

[1]The shell of the cocoanut represents Shaitan (*kāl*) who wishes to keep from
men the blessing contained in the milk and milk-formed flesh of the fruit.

[2]On great occasions there may be as many as 200 present, men and women.
The men sit on one side and the women on the other facing the Mahant, but
come up in any order to receive the *prāsad*. It is said that about a fourth of
those present at the *chaukā* service receive the *Jot Prasād*.

[3]*Jot*, the flame of a candle; *prasād*, consecrated food.

hand which is uppermost a small pill of *Charan Amrita* and a portion of *Parwāna*, and this disposed of receive into the same hand one of the wafers. They then draw near to the Dīwān, who from a brazen vessel pours into the palm of their right hand a few drops of water which they drink. After this they retire to a distance and an attendant pours water over both their hands to cleanse them from contact with their lips. This food is regarded as Kabīr's special gift and it is said that all who receive it worthily will obtain eternal life.

This service is followed by a substantial meal, which is paid for by subscription, should no wealthy member of the Panth have come forward to defray the cost.[1]

After listening to this account of the service I inquired of the Mahant as to the fate of those who abstained from receiving the gifts of Kabīr. He replied that all men on their death-bed could receive from their Mahant *Prasād*, *Charan Amrita* and *Parwāna* and that in cases where the Mahant lived at a distance it was usual to place a certain amount of *Charan Amrita* and *Parwāna* with one or more of his Chelās who could be trusted to keep them safe from all pollution, Such supplies could be utilised at the close af a *Pūran-māṣi chaukā*, when a Mahant was not present, or in cases of serious illness. Every Mahant, he added, kept by him a certain amount of *Prasād*, but he alone could administer or prepare this.

The Mahant explained further that it was only essential that the dying should receive *Charan Amrita* and *Parwāna*; the former testified to the chela's utter devotion to Kabīr, while the latter constituted his passport to the Guru's heavenly mansion.

Upon the death of a member of the *Panth* two cocoanuts are immediately purchased. One of these is carried by the barber in the funeral procession and placed by the side of the dead body, imme-

---

[1]When a Mahant is not present these services are considerably curtailed, as the officiating chelā is only provided with a service book containing a portion of the service nor is he authorised to do all that a Mahant would do. Even when a Mahant is present the service on Sundays is only said in part and is usually brought to a close at midnight. The full service is read at *Pūrana Māsī*. One of my informants told me that there were generally between 30 and 40 present at the Chaukā which he attended on Sundays.

A full *chaukā* service or Ārti Prasād, followed by *Jot Prasād*, can be held at any time, if some one is willing to defray all expenses, including the cost of the meal that follows in accordance with custom.

diately before cremation or burial;[1] the other is kept in the house
and reserved as an offering at the funeral *Chaukā* to be held at
some subsequent date.

The arrangements in connexion with a Funeral Chaukā differ
from those of an ordinary Chaukā in that the awning over the prepared ground is of red instead of white material, a piece of white
cloth is placed over the *chaukā* to represent the dead man's body
and the number of betel leaves is reduced to 124, the leaf removed
representing the dead man's portion.

At the commencement of the service the Mahant prays silently
on behalf of the deceased that he may be preserved from all dan-
gers on his journey. Upon the conclusion of this prayer five funeral
bhajans are sung, after which all present three times do *bandagi* to
the Guru and to the piece of white cloth that represents the body
of the deceased.

The cocoanut which has been specially reserved for this service
is next washed by the Mahant and made over to some relative of
the deceased or, should there be no relative belonging to the Panth,
to some member attached to the same Guru as the deceased. This
man after applying the cocoanut to his forehead, shoulders etc.
returns it with an offering to the Mahant, who breaks it upon a
stone upon which camphor is burning. The rest of the service is
conducted in the manner already described. The number of cocoanuts offered varies from one to nine according to the means of
the friends and relatives. Each cocoanut involves a separate offering to the Mahant. The flesh of the cocoanut or cocoanuts is made
up with flour etc. into small cakes which are sent round to the
houses of Kabīr Panthis by the hands of Bairāgis.

The Religious Orders of Islam

The various orders of Darweshes in Islam correspond in a
measure to the sects of Hinduism. An interesting account of these
Orders will be found in *Essays on Islam* by Canon Sell. From this

---

[1]The bodies of Bairāgis are buried; those of householders, unless they have
received *Bairāg*, are usually cremated.

account it appears that two at least of these Orders were probably established in India previous to the time of Kabīr; the Qādirīyah, founded in 1165, and the Qalandariyah, who were practically Sūfīs and founded in 1232.

The following details in the organisation of these Orders are worthy of attention in connexion with our subject :

1. The extreme respect shown to the Superior of the Order.

"The head of an Order is the spiritual heir of its founder, and is called the Shaikh . . . . He is looked up to with the greatest veneration; in fact-absolute obedience to the Shaikh is the very essence of the system. . . . The adoration of the Master too often takes the place of the worship of God, and the ideal life of a Darwesh is one which is absolute conformity to the will of the Shaikh. Thus, Thou shalt be in the hands of thy Shaikh as a corpse in the hands of those who prepare it for burial. God speaks to thee through him. Thou art his slave and thou canst do nothing without his order. He is a man chosen of God. Banish from thy heart any thought to which God or the Shaikh might object."

2. Branch establishments (Zāwiyah) under the control of a Muqqadim who must be implicitly obeyed by all members of the Order, living in the monastery.

3. The spiritual guide is called a Pīr (Hindu Guru). The ordinary members of the Order are called Ikhwān (Brothers), Aṣhāb (Companions), Murīd (Disciples), or generically Darweshes.

4. There are lay associates, not resident in the monasteries who are in possession of secret signs and words, by use of which they can obtain protection from the community. Lay associates also employ the rosary of the Order.

5. Once or twice a year the Muqaddims meet in conference to consider questions relating to the well-being of the Order. This meeting is called Hazrat; of the use of Huzur as applied by Kabīr Panthis to the Mahant at Headquarters.

6. Novitiates are required to prepare themselves for admission into the Order by fasting, spiritual retreat, prayer and almsgiving.

7. Newly admitted members are said to have entered upon the Tariqā (path, Panth).

8. All members are required to repeat daily a special form of prayer (Zikr).

Hindu Monastic Orders had been previously formed in India by Sankarāchārya, Rāmānuja, Rāmānand etc.

Nānak, a Hindu by birth, was frequently addressed as a Darwesh and associated much with Muhammadans.

EARLY CHRISTIAN INFLUENCES IN NORTHERN INDIA

There have been Christians in Southern India from early days and it is quite possible that Hindu reformers, such as Śankarāchārya and Rāmānuja, came in contact with them. The former was possibly indebted to Christianity for some part of his reforming zeal, while Rāmānuja and his disciple Rāmānand[1] seem also to have been influenced by Christian teaching. From ancient times the more religiously disposed Hindus have been accustomed to visit places of pilgrimage in all parts of the country and when on pilgrimage to converse freely with all who enjoyed a reputation for spiritual enlightenment. Christian thought, in varying degrees of purity, may in this way have penetrated regions unvisited by professing Christians.[2]

The first Roman Catholic missionary to India of whose work we have any account was Friar Jordanus of the Dominican Order. He visited the east in 1321-23 and again in 1330. He mentioned Surat, Baroch and Quilon as places well suited to become centres of Missionary effort. The Inquisition, established at Goa in 1560, punished Muhammadans and other strangers who exercised their religion in the countries subject to the King of Portugal.[3] It is probably to the Inquisition that a Kabīr Panthi refers when, in describing the evils which the Panth was intended to remedy, he writes that at one time religion was so little thought of that a strange people came from the West and made the observance of religious rites a criminal offence, punishable with death.

We do not as yet know much about the work of Christian missi-

---

[1]In describing Rāmānand as a disciple of Rāmānuja I do not wish to imply that the two were contemporaneous. All that is certain is that Rāmānand belonged originally in the School of Rāmānuja.

[2]For further information on this subject see Grierson's lecture on *Modern Hinduism and its Debt to the Nestorians*.

[3]See, *The Syrian Church in India* by G.M. Rae, pp. 187-88, 198.

onaries in Northern India previous to 1570,[1] but we know that the Emperor Akbar in 1579 sent an envoy to the Viceroy of Goa, with a request that he would send to his court some Christian teachers, capable of holding controversy with Muhammadan Mullahs. In response to this request Father Rudolf Aquaviva and two others were despatched to the royal court at Fatehpur Sikri. Rudolf returned to Goa in 1583.[2] At the request of the same Emperor a second deputation, including Hieronymus Xavier a grand nephew of St. Francis Xavier, was sent to Lahore in 1595. For the instruction of non-Christian. Father Xavier wrote several books; *Dastān Masīh* (Life of Christ), *Dastān San Pedro* (Life of St. Peter), and *Aina Haqq nūma* (The Mirror of Truth). *Dastān-i-Masīh* was presented by him to Akbar at Agra in 1602 and subsequently published with a Latin translation by Ludovicus de Dieu in 1639. This work is described as "Historia Christi, sed contaminata." Xavier's work entitled *Aīna Haqq Nūma* was published about 1608 and provoked a reply from Ahmad Ibn Zain to which he gave the name "The Divine rays in refutation of Christian error."[3] Dean Prideaux calls this book "The Brusher of the Glass" and Guadagnoli refers to it as *Politor Speculi.* Guadagnoli possibly made use of an Arabic version of the original Persian. The Jesuits were much alarmed at the appearance of this Muhammadan work and invited some one to answer it without delay. Bonaventura Malvasia, a Franciscan friar of Bononia, replied with *Dilucidatio Specu'i verum monstrantis* in 1628 and Philip Guadagnoli wrote *Apologia pro Christiana religione* which was published in Latin at Rome in 1631 and translated into Arabic in 1637. This latter essay contained many appeals to Popes and Councils which would carry little weight with Muhammadan and Hindu readers.

[1] I am informed that Father Felix is engaged in collecting material for a book that should throw interesting light upon the work of the Roman Church in Northern India, including Kashmir and Tibet.

[2] For further details about Father Rudolf's Mission, see *First Christian Mission to the Great Mughal,* by Father Goldie, published by Gill and Son, Dublin.

[3] I have had an opportunity of examining two interesting publications bearing upon the subject, viz, "Controversial Tracts on Christianity and Muhammadanism" by Henry Martyn, edited by Rev. S Lee, Professor of Arabic in the University of Cambridge and published at the Cambridge University Press in 1824; and a work by Dean Prideaux of Norwich, first published in 1697 entitled "The true nature of imposture, fully displayed in the life of Mahomet". This second work contains an interesting account of all books consulted by the author.

CHAPTER 7

The Teaching of the Panth

IN considering the teaching of Kabīr we confined our attention to two books, the *Bījak* and the *Ādi Granth*. In that case we had practically no choice in the matter; these were the only two books which could be regarded as truly representative of the Guru's teaching. The literature of the Panth is ever on the increase, but the thoughts expressed in most of the writings are very similar.[1] It therefore seems best in this case too to confine our attention to two works which may be regarded as representative of the literature as a whole and to present the reader with an abstract of their teaching. The books selected for this purpose are *Sukh Nidān* and *Amar Mūl*, both of which are closely associated with the Dharam Dāss section of the Panth.

The *Sukh Nidān* is highly spoken of by H.H. Wilson, but we have come across no evidence in support of his statement that its teaching "is only imparted to pupils whose studies are considered to approach perfection."[2] According to Kabīr Panth tradition this book was written about 1729. The character of the language in which it is written, and the subject-matter of the treatise afford evidence in support of this tradition. The *Amar Mūl* is of still later origin, but more representative of the teaching given at the present time to members of the Panth.[3]

---

[1]For a list of the more important writings in connexion with the Panth, p. 6.

[2]Wilson seems to have regarded Dharam Dāss (the servant of religion) as the representative disciple and to have received no information about that section of the Panth which seems in many ways to be the more important of the two.

[3]Each book belonging to the Dharam Dāss section, and practically all the literature does belong to this section, is prefaced by a list of Mahants up to the date of production. This practice should throw considerable light upon the date of production, but its value is neutralised by two circumstances. The MSS. are

Abstruct of Sukh Nidān[1]

Chapter I—The Creator who made all things is king of all. He is the ground, the seed, the root, the branches and the tree itself. Nothing exists apart from him. He has existed in all ages and has admonished all. He is to be found in the heart wherein he has settled. Men have been led astray by Māyā. From the heart of man springs good and evil; charity, faith, righteousness, sin, goodness, nearness, distance, *tīrath* and fasts.

Chapter II—Dharam Dāss was in the habit of worshipping Sālig Rāma. He used to bow down to Bhagats and Bairāgīs and to entertain Sādhus of all kinds. He read the *Bhagawad Gītā* and honoured Gopāla in word and deed. He wore a *tilak* on his forehead and round his neck a mālā of *tulsi* wood. He visited Dwārkā, Jaggannāth, Gayā and Benares, but failed to find rest for his soul. He sang the praises of Rāma and Krishna, but all in vain. When he was at Mattra Kabīr suddenly appeared before him and asked what he had been doing all his life. Dharam Dāss replied that he had been engaged in worshipping the gods and in visiting places of pilgrimage. Kabīr told him that both he and the gods whom he worshipped had been deluded by Māyā; that gods, like Rāma and Krishna who did not even know the hour of their death had no right to be considered omniscient or omnipresent.

Chapter III—Dharam Dāss was at first disgusted by the teaching of Kabīr and thought. 'This low caste man wishes to lead me astray.' He ordered his servant to make a fire that he might prepare food for Sālig Rāma. Dharam Dāss perceived that numberless ants together with their eggs were being consumed in the fire. His heart was touched and he began to think that it was sad that the preparation of food for Sālig Rāma should involve the loss of so much life. Kabīr again appeared before him and rebuked him for his cruelty. He implored him to have mercy upon *Jīvas*, to put out the flame and save as many lives as possible. He once more explained that Rāma, Krishna and Sālig Rāma were no gods and that Rāma himself had been responsible for the loss of many lives.

---

generally so badly written that rhe copyist prefers to copy the list of Mahants from some printed books, while those who do persevere in copying from the original often think it more respectful to the ruling Mahant to bring the list up to date.

[1]For this abstract I am indebted to the Rev. Ahmad Shah.

Kabīr when he saw that Dharam Dāss was much addicted to fasting, rebuked him, saying that without food or rest he could not expect to find God. It was equally futile, he said, to wander about from one place of pilgrimage to another. He should look for one in whose heart was pity and true religion. Dharam Dāss disregarded this advice and continued in his former course.

Chapter IV—Dharam Dāss next visited Benāres and saw there an extraordinary spectacle; learned Pandits and Brahmins worsted in argument by an ordinary man. He thought to himself, "This must be the *Zinda Purush* whom I met before at Mattra." He accordingly asked Kabīr, Who are you? Where do you live? Whom do you worship? Who is the Creator of the world and who is the Master of this life?

Kabīr replies, I am Sat Purush; I am peace and comfort; I am Sukrit; I am Sat Kabīr: I am the Creator of this world. I have created the five elements: I have established three qualities: I am the seed and the tree: I am the possessor of qualities: All are contained in me: I live within all and all live within me.

Dharam Dāss inquires, If you are all things and there is nothing apart from you, how comes it about that there are heaven and hell, Rāma and Krishna, Hindu and Turk ?

Kabīr replies—Your questions are reasonable, but remember earth, air, fire, water and ether are but forms of me: the whole universe is made of these. Therefore I am in all and all is contained in me. Kabīr then in a lengthy speech explained how the universe came into existence. This speech is practically an exposition of certain *Ramainis* and *Shabdas* contained in the *Bijak*.

Chapter V—At the conclusion of this speech Dharam Dāss throws his Sālig Rāma into the river Ganges. He then asked Kabīr how he could be described as *Nirākār* (without form) seeing that he is in all things, acts in all things and speaks in all things. Kabīr explains at length that Māyā has deceived Brahma, Vishnu and Shiva, and that woman has long been notorious for her craftiness. He mourns for his three sons, Brahma, Vishnu, and Shiva, who had been deceived by Māyā, and explains that it is for their sakes, to save them and their descendants, that he has appeared in the world in every age.

Chapter VI—Dharam Dāss asks, "O Zinda Purush, when there were no fields, no trees, no fruits, no herbs, upon what did you live ?" Kabīr explains that his body is immortal and requires no

material food. He again refers to his three sons and the wickedness
of Māyā and relates the efforts made by his sons to remove the
effects of Māyā's evil doing.

Chapter VII—Dharam Dāss next inquires regarding the division
of earth and sky, and the institution of places of pilgrimage. Kabīr
explains that all this is the doing of his three sons whom Māyā
had deceived. He explains the character of the various places of
pilgrimage and the origin of religious sects and caste. Dharam Dāss
asks what orders he has for him, that he may obey them. Kabīr
raplies; My only order for you is that you should save yourself
and save others. He concludes by declaiming against false teachers
and enlarges on the punishments that await their followers.

Chapter VIII—Dharam Dāss gives expression to a difficulty that
perplexes him. Men journey on pilgrimage to every quarter of the
earth, observe fasts and worship the gods, and yet hesitate not to
kill fowls, goats and even cows. What will the end of such men
be? This too, Kabīr explains, is the doing of Māyā. No man can
be saved by mere singing of God's praises, any more than a parrot
can save itself from the cat by singing the praises of God.

Dharam Dāss asks how salvation is to be obtained. Kabīr replies:
Be constant, utter not false words, show love to others, associate
with good people and especially with Sādhus. Gather wisdom from
every source, attend to the wants of holy men: whenever they come
to your house, wash their feet and drink the *Charan Amrita*: feed
them and supply them with every comfort, learn from them whatever of good they can teach you. I am the Sādhu and all Sādhūs
dwell in me. If you meet with a true Sādhu, then your thoughts,
words and deeds will become perfect. There are men who have
disguised themselves as Sādhus, but have no right to the title. Then
Dharam Dāss says, O Sat Guru, now I know that you are the Creator, the true Sādhu and all in all. You are my Master and my place
of pilgrimage. I have only one more question to ask : Those who
confess their faith in you, dwell in you; but those who fail to recognise you or decline to obey your commands, what will be the
end of such men ? What has become of those who in old days
were accounted sages but knew you not ? Kabīr replied, All such
have been rewarded according to their works. Some have become
stars, some insects or moths, some have become plants. Others
have gone to hell and there they will remain for many ages. All
such must pass through 84 lakhs of forms before they can obtain

salvation. Those who believe in me, become absorbed in me.

Dharam Dāss entreats Kabīr to accompany him to his house that he may also instruct his wife and son. When he returned to his house at Bandogarh his wife, Amīnī, asked him why he had been absent so long. He tells her that he has found in Kabīr himself for whom he had been searching so long at places of pilgrimage and bids her also find in him the Creator of the universe, for Kabīr had solved for him all the mysteries of this world. Amīnī says, 'What answer shall I give to your request ? You know that some say that the creator is without form, others that he is to be found in the persons of Rāma or Krishnā. Dharam Dāss relates his own experiences, after which Amīnī too becomes a disciple of Kabīr. Food is prepared and a cocoanut and betel leaf are also brought and Kabīr prepares for them the *Mahā Prasād*.

Abstract of Amar Mūl[1]

Chapter I—Dharam Dāss explains that all the souls in the world are overwhelmed with troubles and implores the Sat Guru to extract with all speed the arrow with which their heart is pierced. In reply to this entreaty the Sat Guru declares that immortality attaches to those into whose heart the immortal Word has entered. To Dharam Dāss's request for an explanation of the mystery of union and separation, the Sat Guru replies that to obtain Mukti an understanding of the Letterless One is necessary with the help of Betel Leaf and the Cocoanut; that the Supreme Being is unconditioned as containing the essence of the Letterless One: conditioned as manifesting the Divine mystery to man; that a true belief in the conditioned and the unconditioned and absorption in the Word are required of all who escape from the power of Yama and the toils of transmigration.

Without a knowledge of the Name none can safely cross the ocean of existence. To four Gurus has it been given to convey souls safely to the Satya Loka (Paradise) and of these four the chief is Dharam Dāss. It is for him and his 42 decendants to rescue souls from the tyranny of Kāl. Of one alone is Kāl afraid and that one is the Word. The spoken word is Māyā; the unutterable name alone is true, the name that pervades all hearts. When the voice of the

---

[1]This abstract was prepared from a translation of *Amar Mūl* made for me by U.R. Clement, Head Master of the Mission School, Indore, and formerly Second Master of the Collegiate School, Cawnpore.

Word was sounded the indestructible one took form. As clouds obstruct the rays of the sun, so does Māyā withhold from man true knowledge. That soul alone attains perfection which learns the secret of the immortal root (*Amar Mul*).

Dharam Dāss presses for a further explanation of the Betel Leaf and the Cocoanut. The Sat Guru replies that the Betel Leaf was not produced in the way of nature but proceeded from the Word, and that the Cocoanut when broken by the true Word is accepted as a substitute for the soul which, as all else in the three Lokas, has been made over by Purusha to Dhamrāe, the Angel of Death. The Cocoanut, the Betel leaf and the Word are the three boats in which souls can safely cross the Ocean of life.

He who would be saved must receive the Betel Warrant, serve the Sādhus with attention and become absorbed in the true Word. This is the secret to be revealed to the wise by Dharm Dāss and his descendants.

Chapter II—The Sat Guru explains that ātma and Brahman are one through union with Paramātma. Ātma stands in the same relation to Paramātma as the wave to the ocean, the spark to the fire and the ornament to the gold out of which it is fashioned. The soul abides in Brahman, as light shines in the rays of the sun. Thus Jīva and Brahman which are commonly regarded as two are really one. Those who have gained this knowledge obtain emancipation.

Dharam Dāss next asks the Sat Guru to explain to him the Letterless One, the bodiless Shabda in the body. The Sat Guru explains that all who have assumed bodies have been produced by Shabda. Shabda is perfect and all else fragmentary. The true Shabda reverberates in the Universe. He who knows the Letterless One finds an abode in Satya Loka. In answer to further inquiries the Sat Guru explains that the splendour of the soul in Satya Loka is equal to that of sixteen suns while the glory of Purusha himself is indescribable. The true name is the basis of the soul. By a draught of nectar doubts are removed and the thirst of ages satisfied. All the souls in Satya Loka see with the feelings of love and never give utterance to unkind thoughts. Hope and desire find no place there. The sins of millions of births are washed away by the influence of Name. Without the Name all efforts are in vain; without the Name knowledge is of no account. As darkness prevails where there is no lamp, so is there darkness in the heart that is without the Name.

Chapter III—To reach the Ocean of Bliss souls must serve the Satgur and so banish the fear of all, they must receive the sacramental food and render acceptable service to their Guru; they must promote the happiness of others and recognise that the Guru is identical with the Lord: they must be simple-minded and drink the water in which Sādhus have washed their feet; they must never speak ill of their Guru and meditate on the love of the Letterless One; they must remember the Name day and night, and place no trust in the illusion of Karma. He who knows the Name is of the family of Dharam Dāss, The *Veda* knows not the extent of the Name. All declare, 'We know not, we know not'. The Pandit reads and gropes in the dark; he knows not the existence of the Ādi Brahman. The acquisition of knowledge produces pride and is of no use in the hour of death. Eighteen *Puranas* have been written and of these the *Bhāgawata* is the best. It explains the glory of Brahman and establishes the efficacy of devotion. Fools read, but to no purpose; they think not of that which is obtainable through the intellect. Those only obtain wisdom who fall in with the Sat Guru. Of what use is the boat without the boatman?

He who knows the secret of the rosary is absorbed in the true Name. Welcome the secret that overcomes fear in all three forms, physical, mental and spiritual. Escape thus from the halter of many births.

Doubt, the angel of Kāl, has taken up his abode in the hearts of men. Doubt is the offspring of Dharma. He who understands the letterless one banishes doubt and enters into the house of immortality. Only through a knowledge of the Name can doubt be banished from the heart.

Dharam Dāss urges that but few Jīvas possess knowledge. How then can the world escape destruction ?

The Sat Guru replies, I impart to you the secret of him that possesses knowledge. The *Hansa* that receives the Betel warrant will undoubtedly attain Nirvāṇa. He in whose heart there is belief will safely cross the ocean of rebirths. After receiving the Betel he will speak the truth. He will keep the feet of the Satgur in his heart. He will sacrifice all for the Satgur and attend to the needs of the saints. He will banish all fondness for sons and wife and forsake all for the feet of the Satgur. He will wash his feet and drink of the washings. So in the hereafter will he drink nectar in Satya Loka. Dharam Dāss inquires whether women also can obtain salvation.

The Sat Guru replies: Women also can cross the ocean by faith in the Name. Women are without knowledge, therefore they must offer their body, mind and wealth to the Sants, and serve them devotedly. If they despise the Sants they will fall into the snare of Dhamrāe. Those women can escape the noose of Kāl who offer all at the feet of the Guru and serve him day and night.

The Sat Guru exhorts Dharam Dāss to shake off illusion and teach to men devotion, for on him has been placed the burden of the world and it is his seal that will be everywhere respected. To him too has been entrusted the touchstone by means of which crows (*jīvas*) can be converted into swans (*hansas*). Through the vehicle of the Name the shape and colour of the Jīva can be changed.

Chapter IV—Dharam Dāss inquires into the meaning of the touchstone and is told that it varies in the case of individuals. In the case of the wise it is to be found in a knowledge of Shabda, in the case of children in the reception of the Betel leaf, and in the case of the passionate in devotion.

After all these explanations the Sat Guru is angered when Dharam Dāss asks how it is possible for the Sant to live in this world, and disappears from view. Dharam Dāss is much distressed and cries, "Be merciful, O Lord, the perfect Guru. I knew not that you could read the heart; through ignorance I failed to understand your teaching. In my pride I erred; pardon my fault. O Guru, you are the true Guru; like unto Brahman I was very proud, but when a child speaks foolishly its parents hasten to forget its foolishness. O Lord, the merciful one, have pity on me now. If you do not reveal yourself to me again, I will destroy my life. It was you who imparted to me this religion, therefore I put to you that question." Kabīr had pity on Dharam Dāss and again appeared before him. The joy of Dharam Dāss was as that of the Chakor when it beholds the moon.

He held fast to the feet of the Guru and worshipped him; he washed his feet and drank of the water in which they had been washed. Then he prayed, "O Lord, give unto thy servant *Mahāprasād*".

At the bidding of Dharam Dāss Amīnī prepared a plentiful repast and Ārti was offered in a golden vessel. The wife of Dharam Dāss and all his children fell at the Guru's feet and drank the water in which they had been washed. All listened to the words of divine knowledge. The Lord Kabīr sat at the Chaukā. After Kabīr had eaten and washed, he offered Prasād to Dharam Dāss and all those who were present. All that were in the house were filled with joy.

Then Amīnī prepared a bed upon which the Sat Guru took his seat. Dharam Dāss fanned him, while Amīnī shampooed his feet. All the Sants adored him. Then Amīnī said, Lord, I offer in thy service this body of mine, my heart, my wealth and all that I possess. Do as it pleaseth thee. Then the Lord took her by the hand and set her beside him on the bed. He tested her and placed his hand kindly on her head and said, Amīnī, go your way, I see that your mind is chaste. The mind leads one to do good and bad actions, and makes the body act according to its pleasure. For your sake I have renounced all desires of the flesh.

The Sat Guru then renewed his promises to Dharam Dāss assuring him that he should have forty-two generations of children in whose hands would rest the salvation of the world.

Dharam Dāss said, "O Lord, grant unto my descendants this blessing that through them souls may be set free. This is my prayer, that my descendants may be accounted as yours; then all will be saved."

The Sat Guru replied, "In the world the Hansas will be set free by the hands of thy descendants. The children of thy generations shall be welcomed as a touchstone. They will be free from the disturbance of passion, their minds will be absorbed in the contemplation of Shabda, their mode of living will be serious and collected; their thoughts and words will be directed towards the truth; they will have a knowledge of self and subtle things. He is my descendant who knows Shabda. How can he be saved who makes distinctions in the touchstone ? I have revealed the path to you, but remember that there is no sin so great as that of hiding the path of salvation. Those who know the word should proclaim it in various countries and liberate all Hansas that have intelligence. None can be saved without the Name. All who are without the Name are proud. Very few have experience of the Name. Dharam Dāss, remember, I am day and night with him who knows the Name."

Chapter V—The Sat Guru explains that Dhamrāe had objected to his coming into the world to save souls since all three Lokas had been made over to him by Purusha, and had asked by what name he hoped to liberate the Hansas. All who performed religious acts were in his power, including Shiva, as he sat with pride in *Samādhi*; in the great day of destruction all would be destroyed by him, even Vishṇu, the greatest of all. Gyāni had replied that Dhamrāe had acted as a thief, seeking to establish his authority where he had no right to rule and that for this reason he had been sent forth to rescue souls by Purusha, the true God. with whom Dhamrāe had vainly striven to identify himself. Dhamrāe had implored Gyāni to be king to him, even as Purusha had been kind. but that Gyāni had only consented to leave him undisturbed on condition that he would promise not to approach those who had received the Betel leaf, to treat with kindness all who had become Gyāni and to show love to all who had welcomed Shabda. Dhamrāe had accepted this offer but had at the same time been warned that his rule would come to an end so soon as Shabda had become established in the world.

Dharam Dāss thanks the Sat Guru for having thus cooled the lotus of his heart, and asks for a fuller account of Kāl.

The Sat Guru explains that Kāl is the cause of all actions in this world, that he has deceived the ten Avatāra of Vishnu, is the cause of virtue and vice, is in reality a form assumed by Purusha and has power over all but Shabda. Kāl is the author of that duality which exists wherever the true Word has not been apprehended. *Yog, jap, tap*, sacrifice and alms-giving all have their origin in a fear of Kāl. Kāl is an embodiment of selfishness; he devours all who live a life of enjoyment. Through Kāl creation has come into existence and in Kāl it will fade away.

In reply to an inquiry as to which was first, Purusha or Kāl, the Sat Guru explains that first was space, and that in that space Purusha produced Shabda from Shabda, that space and time (Kāl) were really one, but that so terrible was Kāl that none dare look upon his face. But for the noose of Kāl there had been no need for devotion. Only through a knowledge of the Name could the fear of Kāl be overcome.

Chapter VI—In connexion with an account of the Chaukā Dharam Dāss asks for how many sins a cocoanut should be broken and is told that a cocoanut is broken for sins a lakh and a quarter in number. He is also told that the splitting of the straw will wash away the sins of many births.

The following Mantras are prescribed:

1. *At the time of drinking water*—Immortal tank and transparent water. The Hansa drinks to his satisfaction. The body is gold, the mind is blissful, the fear of Karma is effaced.

2. *At the time of bathing*—The water of Sat Sukrit was brought in. The child of Dhani bathed. He directed his attention to the feet of the Lord. Kabīr says—Hear, Dharam Dāss, in the beginning and the end there exists an abode of blazing flame. The immortal name is peaceful. In fourteen mansions and nine apartments there is one true Kabīr.

3. *At the time of taking food*—The Chaukā is made of the word that removes fear; purification is the result of satisfaction and good character. There is the light of love and faith; Sat Sukrit began to dine. When the name of Sat Sukrit was pronounced, the water became sacred, giving joy to the Sants. All the Sants united to produce light. Father Kabīr began to eat and the wealthy Dharam Dāss was taking his food. Then all the Sants took Prasād. The saved enjoyed the absence of fear.

Dharam Dāss makes inquiry as to what is necessary for the proper performance of Ārtī. He is told that in the first place the house should be whitewashed. There should be provided seven cocoanuts, thirty and a quarter maunds of sweet meats of eight different kinds, three and a quarter pounds of sugar candy, twelve thousand betel leaves and a plentiful supply of sandal wood, camphor, cloves, betel nuts and cardamums. A silk dhoti should be provided for the officiating Mahant. the canopy over the *chaukā* should be made of gold cloth and the vessel in which the dew is collected should be of gold.

Whoever celebrates an Ārtī after this manner will pass immediately to Satya Loka, provided that it is not celebrated from any selfish motive.

Dharam Dāss urges that in this Kali Yuga men are poor and very few could afford to celebrate an Ārtī on so liberal a scale,

The Sat Guru replies that a simpler form is permissible. In this three and a quarter pounds of sweets, one cocoanut and a hundred betel leaves will suffice, but a new Dhoti must be provided for the Mahant and an offering of money made by all present to the Sat Guru.

He further adds that when the *Kadhār* (disciples) are not in a position to celebrate the Ārtī once a month, it will be sufficient to celebrate it twice in the year, in the months of *Phāgun* (February) and of *Bhādon* (August).

In conclusion the Sat Guru warns Dharam Dāss that the Guru who celebrates the Ārtī must have a knowledge of the letter, otherwise both he and his disciples will find themselves in Hell (Jam-Loka).

Chapter VII—The Sat Guru discourses on the four castes.

The special duty of the *Brahmin* is to gain a knowledge of Brahman. He in vain repeats the *Gyātrī*, performs *Sandhyā* and reads the *Vedas*, if he is devoid of knowledge. Why do he Brahmins confine their attention to Sanskrit? Is the vernacular unsuited to spiritual instruction? The Brahmins in pride of heart despise the Sādhus who are true seekers after God and taunt them with having given up caste for the sake of their stomachs. Those who know not Brahman and neglect to practise devotion cannot obtain salvation.

The special duties of the *Kshatriya* are to protect cows, Brahmins and women. But in an age when cows are slaughtered, Brahmins draw their own water and men commit adultery, of what use are the Kshatriyas ? They commit murder and receive the praise of men, but the true Kshatriya is he who exercises forbearance and has true sympathy with others.

The special duties of the *Vaishya* are to have pity upon the hungry and to go on pilgrimage, but it is vain to strain water before drinking, in the desire to save life, if there is no faith in Hari. Those who indulge in sensuality fall into the power of Yamarāj, and in vain worship Pārasnāth, the great, wise Guru, when they disregard his counsel. Let all such fall at the feet of the Sat Guru and learn the secret of the Name.

The *Śūdra* whose duty it is to render service has discovered the Bhakti of the Satgur. He serves the Brahmin and has cast forth from his heart all desires of the flesh, anger and avarice. He serves also the Kshatriyas and the Vaishyas and is well spoken of in Brahma Loka. Other castes neglect their duties, but the Śūdra prostrates himself at the feet of the Sat Guru and so finds his way to Satya Loka.

Dharam Dāss, you are a Śūdra by caste, but all who honour the water of your feet will escape from the ocean of rebirths. The soul that is born a Śūdra is saved, if it meditates on Brahman. Kāl in vain attacks the soul that knows the mystery of Shabda.

Dharam Dāss says, Lord, through you I have obtained Mukti, but why has not my family also obtained it ?

The Sat Guru explains that his descendants up to the eighth generation will be tainted with pride, treat with contumely men who bear the name of Kabīr, and seek honour in the world instead of placing reliance on the Name.

Those who practise true Bhakti save themselves and others, spend all that they have in feeding Sādhus. speak the truth to all, cherish the true name in their hearts suffer not feelings of anger to arise, speak under the influence of the Name, reason about knowledge and preach the doctrine of Shabda.

In the eighth generation will be born a child who will bring men back into the true Path.[1] The Jiva that finds the immortal Name loses all fear. I dwell in the heart in which the immortal Shabda shines. Regrets will be the portion of him who finds not the immortal Name.

Chapter VIII—Dharam Dāss gives expression to his belief that the Purusha dwells in the Guru and that there is no distinction between the Guru and the Purusha. The Sat Guru again describes the work assigned to Dharam Dāss and his descendants. Dharam Dāss says that with the permission of the Guru he will send all the children (disciples) to Satya Loka. The Sat Guru reminds him that there are two kinds of children, those of the flesh and those of the spirit, and that the spiritual children are those who cherish the name of the Sat Guru. The time will come, he adds, when all creation will enter Satya Loka and all animate beings become absorbed in the Satgur.

Dharam Dāss urges that the work of saving souls belongs to the Sat Guru and he himself might well be relieved of so great responsibility. This the Satgur declines to do.

Dharam Dāss inquires why he, being the Purusha, had visited this mortal world. The Satguru speaks of the time when there was neither space nor non-space, neither sin nor righteousness, neither Shesha (serpent) nor Kāl, neither the seven days of the week nor the fifteen days of the lunar month, when Brahma, Vishnu and Shiva had no existence. Then the Ādi Purusha produced the world through Shabda and Shabda produced intelligence, Finally Kāl was brought into existence and began to persecute the Jivas. Purusha perceiving this had pity upon them and sent the Satgur to rescue them from the clutches of Kāl.

He compares Purusha to a child who builds a house and then destroys it and afterwards runs crying to his mother, saying. "Build

---

[1]Are we to infer from this statement that *Amar Mūl* was written when the eighth Mahant was on the gaddi?

again for me my house." Such is the sport of Purusha. He is foolish
and he is wise, he is proud and he is humble, he is true and he is
false. Such teaching is only for those who have the power to understand.

Dharam Dāss asks for an explanation of Ātma Gyān that all the
Hansas may obtain salvation. The Sat Guru explains that he who
has divine knowledge will understand that the Guru and the Chelā
are one. So also the enemy and the friend are one. Himself is active
and himself is passive; himself shows and himself sees; himself
causes birth and death, and himself is death; himself is the image
and himself the worshipper; himself is the branch and himself is
the tree; himself is all manifest and himself is hidden in himself.

But why, Dharam Dāss asks, why if all is equivalent to Brahman,
does the Jiva remain in ignorance? The Sat Guru explains that
Brahman is the seed out of which all things are developed and that
the Shabda is of subtle form: that the Jiva is in Brahman as the
wave is in the sea, the ray of light in the sun, oil in the oil-seed
and the scent in the flower.

Such is the relation of Ātma to Paramātmā.

Chapter IX—The Sat Guru explains that all sense of duality is
due to Māyā, that when man knows himself he becomes himself,
and when he realises himself he becomes Brahman. Until he knows
himself he weeps and cries, and wades through the swamp of
delusion.

The light of knowledge shines forth when Brahman abides in the
heart. Then *Karma* and *Dharma* are obliterated; then there is neither
coming nor going. As it was, so it is, and all intervening delusion
disappears. All apparent contradictions are reconciled in the fulness
of knowledge. Brahman himself is the Word that cannot be uttered,
and himself the Word that speaks to all; himself is formless and
himself is all the forms; he is both *Nirguṇa* and *Saguṇa*. Dharam
Dāss is warned that he must first purify his own heart and mind
before he can so preach to others that they can obtain *Mukti* and
escape from the toils of transmigration. All reasonings and religious writings are the work of Māyā; what is required is devotion
and *Tattwa-gyān*, (the knowledge of essentials). All delusion
(*Bharma*) is removed through meditation.

The Sat Guru explains that he was once in Satya Loka, or rather
beyond it, and that he then saw what is indescribable; that the
form of Purusha was wonderful, to be imagined, not described;

that the abodes in Satya Loka were innumerable and that in all Hansas was discernible the one letter. In the Loka of Kabīr he saw the forms of many Kabīrs, but looking again he saw that it was but one form multiplied. In the light of the true Shabda all is one, there is no second.

The people of the world are taught by means of stories, but for those who understand, all such stories fall far short of the truth. All apparent distinctions are the creation of the mind. He who knows the letter thoroughly suffers no duality to enter into his mind. The only difference between Brahman and Jīva is this, that the latter is the reflection of the former.

Chapter X—The Sat Guru instructs Dharam Dāss to act thus in the case of one who wishes to become a disciple. In the first place he should give him betel, then, if he seems to possess *gyān*, reveal to him the majesty of Shabda, and when his faith in Shabda is confirmed impart to him profound knowledge. Ātmārām abides in the heart of him who has full knowledge. When Ātmārām is realised, he himself is Ātmārām; he knows no second.

The Sat Guru tells how once when he was in Satya Loka Purusha appeared to him and said, "Kabīr, you and I are one; entertain no thought of duality. I am in you and my form is in all the earth. There are eighty-four lakhs of species and I live in all. Beside me there is no second. All creation is delusion. All the countless gods and sages, even Brahma himself, are entangled in delusion." Dharam Dāss rejoins, "O Guru, this is your statement. Is there not need of a second witness?" The Sat Guru replies that he made this statement in the Tretā age, and that Madhukⁿr, Brahmin, is the second witness. He continues, "Kabīr is in all bodies; the speaker is Shabda. There is one form and one Shabda. There is only one form, and ore Shabda. There is only one form, one Shabda and one Purusha, manifest in all. He who knows one is one; the second is this world."

Dharam Dāss asks how it is that Jīvas fail to realise their unity with Brahman. The Sat Guru replies, All the Jīvas came from Brahm-Loka undefiled and devoid of Karma. The clouds lift up the water from the ocean and rain down pure water, but in contact with the earth the water becomes impure. Then is the Jīva embraced by Māyā; the body at birth is defiled by Karma. As the air purifies the impure water, so does *Gyān* remove Karma and the purity of the Jīva is restored. Knowing itself, it separates itself from the water and being disembodied reaches the Durbār. The Ātmā mingles with Paramātmā, as the rivers flow into the ocean. Only in this way can Paramātmā be found. The Ātmā without Shabda is blind and cannot find the path. He who sees Ātmārām is present everywhere; all he sees is like himself, there is nought else beside Brahman. "I am he, I am he; the true Kabīr."

Literature on the Life and Teaching of Kabīr

Names printed in italics refer to writings that exist in manuscript only. In the case of printed books, the place of publication is added within brackets. An asterisk is prefixed to the names of manuscripts known only by hearsay.

1. *Achhar Bhed kī Ramainī.*
2. *Achhar Khand kī Ramainī.*
3. *Agādh Mangal.*
4. *Āgam Ujiyār.*
5. *Alif Nāmā.* (1)
6. *Alif Nāmā.* (2)
7. *Alif Nāmā.* (3)
8. *Allāh Tok.*
9. *Amar Mūl.*
10. Ambu Sāgar. (Bombay)
11. Anū Rāg Sāgar. (Bombay)
12. *Asār Grāhi ko ang.*
13. *Ātam Anubhau.*
14. *Balakh Paij.*
15. *Bhaktī ko ang.*
16. *Bhau Tāran.*
17. *Bhopāl Bodh.*
18. *Bārah Māsā.*
19. *Basant.*
20. Bījak with commentary by Rājā of Rewah. (Lucknow, Benares and Bombay)
21. Bījak with commentary by Puran Dāss. (Lucknow and Allahabad)
22. Bījak with notes by Rev. Prem Chand. (Calcutta)
23. *Chauka kī Ramainī.*
24. *Chauntisi.*

25. *Garur Bodh.*
26. *Gaurī.*
27. *Gorakh Gusht.*
28. Gur Updesh. (Bombay)
29. *Gyān Dīpak.*
30. *Gyān Godrī.*
31. Gyān Sāgar. (Bombay)
32. *Hansāwalī.*
33. *Hanūmān Bodh.*
34. *Hori.*
35. *Hari Rām Līlā.*
36. Kabīr Charitra Bodh. (Bombay)
37. Kabīr Kasauti. (Bombay)
38. Kabīr Manshūr. (Bombay)
39. Kabīr Upāsnā. (Bombay)
40. Kabīr Sāhib kī Sākhī. (Lucknow)
41. *Kamāl Gusht.*
42. *Karnī Binā Kathnī ko aṅg.*
43. *Karni Sahit Kathnī ko aṅg.*
44. *Kūsangit ko aṅg.*
45. *Kurmaulī.*
46. *Madad Bodh.*
47. *Mangal.*
48. *Muktī Māl.*
49. *Muhammad Bodh.*
50 Mūl Ramainī. (Lucknow)
51. *Mūsā Bodh.*
52. *Nām Mahātam.*
53. *Nānak Gusht.*
54. *Niranjan Gusht.*
55. *Nirbhai Gyān.*
56. *Piya Pahchan ko aṅg.*
57. *Puno Mahātam.*
58. *Rāmānand Gusht.*
59. *Rekhtā.*
60. *Sādhu ko aṅg.*
61. *Sam Darsī ko aṅg.*
62. *Samjhe Ghāt ko aṅg.*
63. Santokh Bodh. (27 writings, Bombay)
64. *Sarab Gyātā ko aṅg.*

65. *Sar Grāhi ko aṅg.*
66. Sar Sangrah Prishnotar. (Lucknow)
67. *Sarawag Saugar Sanyukt.*
68. *Sat Kabīr kī Sākhī.*
69. Sat Kabīr kī Shatak Satik. (Benares)
70. *Sat Sang ko aṅg.*
71. *Sat Sang Mahima ko aṅg.*
72. *Shabd Bhawani.*
73. *Shabd Chauntisi.*
74. *Shabd Pukar.*
75. *Sikandar Bodh.
76. *Sowansa Gunjar.*
77. *Sukh Nidhan.*
78. *Sukrit Dhyān.*
79. Ugr Gitā. (Lucknow)
80. *Vasist Muni Gusht.
81. Vivek Sāgar. (Bombay)
82. *Vivek Sangrām.*

In addition to the above H.H. Wilson in *Essays on the Religion of the Hindus*, vol. I, pp. 76-7 mentions:

Ānand Rām Sāgar.
Bālakh kī Ramainī.
Chancharas.
Hindolas.
Jhūlanas.
Kabīr Panji.
Kaharas.
Shabdāwalī.

Pandit Walji Bhai

Pandit Walji Bhai, who worked for many years as a Pastor of the Irish Presbyterian Church at Borsad in the district of Khaira in Gujarat, devoted much time to a study of literature connected with the Kabīr Panth and the religion of the Sikhs. The Pandit was led to believe that the Kabīr Panth was instituted by Jesuits and found confirmation of this belief in the secrecy observed by members of the Panth regarding their literature and teaching.

In 1881 he published in Gujarati under the name *Kabīr Charitra* an exposition of his views upon the subject which he has elsewhere summarised thus:

1. In Kabīr's book it is written that when the first woman Eve, being deceived, repented of her sin, God promised that from her sex a great Man will be born and He shall overcome Satan and save His people.

2. According to the promise, God sent His Son to save the world. This Son lived with God as Word from the beginning, and at the appointed time became flesh to save His people and was called Kabīr.

3. He was tempted by Satan

4. At last He was nailed to a tree and suffered agony

5. God's Son took the burden of His people upon Himself.

6 God's Son worked miracles.

7. God's Son rose from the dead.

8. After God's Son rose from the dead He commanded His disciples to go to all countries and preach the Gospel.

9 God's Son ascended into heaven.

10. In Kabīr's books baptism and the Lord's Supper are commanded to be observed. Generally, all the doctrines of the Bible are to be found in Kabīr's books.

He further held that Nānak, the disciple of Kabīr, was also influenced by Christian teaching and that Hari, the name given to the Sat Guru in the *Ādi Granth*, was used as a synonym for Christ. He worked out his theory with great industry and published the results of his studies in two small volumes, *Hari Charitra* and *A Key to the Ādi Granth*.[1]

I had some interesting correspondence with the Pandit which was only interrupted by his death in December 1903.

The Pandit's writings are not marked by any great critical acumen. Many of his interpretations may be regarded as far-fetched, while his suggested derivations of words are often more ingenious than convincing. His main position is undermined by the assumption that Kabīr is responsible for all literature connected with the Panth. In spite, however, of these defects he has much to say that is both interesting and suggestive. Would that more Indian Christians would study the religious beliefs of their country with equal industry and enthusiasm, and that all Indian Clergy were as diligent as he in studies that result in a more perfect understanding of the Scriptures!

[1]Both these books were printed at the Presbyterian Mission Press, Ludhiana, Panjab.

Glossary

Achhar—letter of the alphabet.
Agādh—deep, unfathomable.
Agam—unfathomable.
Ākāśa—the fifth element, ether.
Alif-nāmā—account of Arabic alphabet.
Amar—immortal.
Ambu—perception, mind.
Amrita—immortal (drink), nectar.
Ānand—happiness.
Anūrāg—desire.
Ārti—sacrificial offering of light.
Ātmā—soul.
Bairāg—renunciation of the world.
Bandagī—service, respectful salutation as from a slave to his master.
Bārah—twelve.
Basant—tune or hymn associated with the season of spring.
Batāsa—small wafer, made of sugar
Be-dharm—without religion.
Bhajan—hymn, sung as an act of worship.
Bhakti—devotion.
Bhawānī—wife of Shiva. Shabd Bhawānī, a morning hymn.
Bhau—fear.
Bhed—secret, mystery.
Bodh—knowledge.
Bunmah—shop-keeper.
Chāncharā—an evening hymn.
Charitra—picture, biography.
Chaukā—square space, specially prepared for the consumption of food.
Chauntisī—Thirty-four, letters of Hindi alphabet.
Chelā—disciple, in relation to spiritual guide Guru.
Dāl—the split grain of certain kinds of pulse.

Dhotī—a cloth, tied round the waist and falling over the legs.

Dhyān—attention to.

Dīpak—lamp.

Durbār—a royal levee, the judgement hall of God.

Garur—a mythical bird, mentioned in the Rāmāyaṇa.

Gauri—a musical measure.

Ghāt—mind.

Ghāt—flight of steps, leading down to the river; used for religious bathing, for the cremation of the dead etc.

Ghī—clarified butter.

Godri—a patch-work coat, worn by *sādhus*.

Gunjār—echo.

Gusht—dialogue, controversy.

Gyān—wisdom.

Gyānī—possessed of wisdom.

Gyātā—wise.

Gyātrī—a sacred verse from the *Ṛgveda*, used by Brahmins and others in their morning devotions.

Hansā—goose, used figuratively for the soul of man, as never abiding in one place.

Hindola—hymn, sung while swinging in a sitting position.

Hori—a musical mode, used during the Holi, a spring festival.

Jam—the angel of death.

Jāneo—the sacred thread worn over the left shoulder by members of the twice-born castes; the Brahmins, the Kshattriyas and the Vaishyas.

Jap—the mumbling of prayers or other devotional exercises.

Jhūlana—hymn sung while swinging, in a standing position.

Jīva—soul, life.

Kadhār—disciple.

Kāfir—unbeliever, from a Muhammadan point of view.

Kaharā—a musical mode.

Kāl—time, death.

Kaṇthi—a necklace, made generally of fruit seeds or wooden beads.

Karma—action as involving punishment or reward.

Kasauti—touchstone.

Khand—group, division.

Kusangit—associating with wicked persons.

Lākh—number, 100,000.

Langoti—loin-cloth.

Līlā—play, drama.
Loka—world.
Mahā—prefix = great.
Mahātam—greatness.
Māla—rosary.
Maṅgal—joy, hymn of praise.
Mantra—a verbal formula, used for religious or semi-religious pur-
    poses.
Manshūr—spreading abroad, publication.
Māsa—month.
Math—monastic building.
Mukti—liberation, salvation.
Mūl—root.
Nidāhn—mansion, abode.
Niranjan—void of passions, a title applied to God by Kabīr Panthis.
Nirbhai—without fear.
Nirguṇa—without qualities.
Pahchān—knowledge.
Paij—entry.
Pān—betel leaf.
Panch Māl—rosary with five strings.
Pānde—a high caste Brahmin.
Panji—path.
Param-ātmā—the great, all-pervading soul.
Parameshwar—the great God.
Parwānā—authoritative document, passport.
Pir—Muhammadan saint.
Piyā—husband.
Prasād—offering made to God.
Prishnottar—question-answer, catechism.
Pukār—call.
Puno—the day of full moon.
Puno Granth—form of service used at *Puran Māsi*.
Puran Māsi—the festival of full moon.
Purush—being, person.
Ramaini—a short exposition of religious truth.
Rekhta—Poetry, written in a mixed dialect (Hindi, Urdu, Persian,
    Arabic etc.)
Sādhu—a Hindu monk.
Sāgar—sea.

Saguṇa—with qualities.

Sākat—man of the world, unspiritual.

Samādhi— the tomb of a holy man.

Samādhi—the condition of one completely absorbed in religious
        meditation.

Sam Darsi—concentration of attention on one object.

Samjhe—understanding.

Sāndhya—the meeting of day and night; a form of devotion used
        at that time.

Sangrāh—protection.

Sangrām—battle, controversy.

Sanyukt—union.

Sār—whole.

Sarab—complete.

Sarawag—whole.

Sat-sang—association with good men.

Satya—true.

Shabda—a word or saying; the word of God. also see p. 43.

Shaikh—a Muhammadan priest.

Shāstras—a code of laws, the Hindu scriptures.

Shatah—one hundred approximately.

Smriti—memory, religious teaching based upon tradition.

Somtokh—contentment.

Sowansa—breath.

Sūdra—a Hindu, not belonging to one of the three twice-born castes.

Sukh—peace.

Sukrit—virtuous.

Swāmi—a Hindu religious teacher, held in great respect by his dis-
        ciples.

Tap—the practice of religious austerities.

Tāran—enabling to cross (river or ocean).

Tilak—a sect mark, usually worn upon the forehead.

Tinkā—straw.

Tinkā-Arpan—the offering of straw in sacrifice the name given to
        the initiatory service in the Kabīr Panth.

Tīrtha—a place of pilgrimage.

Tok—atom.

Ugrā—a title of Shiva.

Ujiyār—light.

Upāsnā—fasting.

Updesh—teaching.
Vivek—discrimination.
Yama—the angel of death.
Yoga—religious meditation.
Yuga—age in the world's history.
Zindā—living.

Index